HOW MUCH FREEDOM MUST WE FORGO TO BE FREE?

A Convoco Edition

CORINNE MICHAELA FLICK (ED.)

Convoco! Editions

Copyright © for the texts by the authors
and Convoco Foundation 2022

The rights of the named authors to be identified as the authors of this work have been asserted in accordance with the Copyright, Designs and Patents Act, 1988.

The publisher has used its best endeavors to ensure that the URLs for external websites referred to in this book are correct and active at the time of going to press. However, the publisher has no responsibility for the websites and can make no guarantee that a site will remain live or that the content is or will remain appropriate.

Convoco Foundation
Brienner Strasse 28
D – 80333 Munich
www.convoco.co.uk

British Library Cataloguing-in-Publication data: a catalogue record for this book is available from the British Library.

Edited by Dr. Corinne Michaela Flick
Translated from German by Philippa Hurd
Layout and typesetting by Jill Sawyer Phypers
Printed and bound in Great Britain by Clays Ltd., St Ives plc

ISBN: 978-1-9163673-4-0

Previously published Convoco titles:

New Global Alliances: Institutions, Alignments and Legitimacy in the Contemporary World (2021)

The Standing of Europe in the New Imperial World Order (2020)

The Multiple Futures of Capitalism (2019)

The Common Good in the 21st Century (2018)

Authority in Transformation (2017)

Power and its Paradoxes (2016)

To Do or Not To Do—Inaction as a Form of Action (2015)

Dealing with Downturns: Strategies in Uncertain Times (2014)

Collective Law-Breaking—A Threat to Liberty (2013)

Who Owns the World's Knowledge? (2012)

Can't Pay, Won't Pay? Sovereign Debt and the Challenge of Growth in Europe (2011)

On my schoolboy's notebook
On my desk and on the trees
On the sand on the snow
I write your name

On all the pages read
On all the blank pages
Stone blood paper ash
I write your name

...

And by the power of a word
My life returns to me
I am born again to know you
And to name you

Liberty.

Paul Éluard, Liberty (1942)

We must keep freedom to its word
and give the word its freedom.

Albert Ostermaier (Convoco Forum 2021)

CONTENTS

	Introduction	1
	Theses	13
1.	The Economic Consequences of Restricting Freedoms during the COVID-19 Pandemic Clemens Fuest	21
2.	Competition as a Guarantor of Freedom Monika Schnitzer	41
3.	Internal Freedom: The Fox and the Hedgehog Timo Meynhardt	59
4.	Freedom of Speech and Freedom of Thought Tim Crane	77

5. Are Human Freedom and Autonomy 91
   Just an Illusion?
   Herbert A. Reitsamer

6. Autonomy and Protection— 109
   Ambivalences in Fundamental Rights
   Stefan Korioth

7. Sustainability as a Prerequisite of 125
   Personal and Entrepreneurial Freedom
   Hildegard Wortmann

8. Freedom and the Tensions between 141
   Collective Values: A Historical Perspective
   on the 19th Century
   Jörn Leonhard

9. Individual and Social Dimensions of 159
   Freedom and Liberty
   Birke Häcker

10. How Much Freedom Must we Forgo to 189
    be Free? Security and Freedom are
    Interdependent
    Bruno Kahl

11. The Dangers of the New Superpower 205
    Rivalry between the US and China
    Peter Wittig

12. Is the Rise of China Endangering our Freedom? 219
    Gabriel Felbermayr

13. The European Model of Freedom in System Conflict: Under Stress and Put to the Test 237
    Sven Simon

14. Freedom, Equality, Democracy 251
    Claudia Wiesner

15. Freedom and Taxes 271
    Rudolf Mellinghoff

16. Freedom out of the Passion for Order: A Minimally Invasive Autopsy of Liberalism 281
    Bazon Brock

17. Freedom, Rhythms, and Restriction 287
    Hans Ulrich Obrist and Martha Jungwirth in Conversation

18. Freedom in the Anthropocene 301
    Philipp Pattberg

    Contributors 317

INTRODUCTION

Dear Friends of Convoco,

In July 2021 we asked the Convoco! network the following question: "Has the pandemic changed your views on freedom?" Of those surveyed 73 percent answered yes.[1] The pandemic has made me recognize how much freedom is a core value for me. I realized how much I like being German and European and living in Europe with its open borders.

Which Institutions Guarantee our Freedom?

In Germany, as in most Western countries, individual freedoms are anchored in the Constitution, in the Basic Law [*Grundgesetz*]. Fundamental rights are the individual's rights of defense against the state. They guarantee that I can rely on being able to lead my life in freedom. After World War II, in 1948, Germany put its trust in the principle of freedom and thereby on the individual's power to act. Self-help based on freedom was the point of departure for putting life in society back on track.[2] At the same time, fundamental rights are the core of the free democratic system, because "democracy is freedom's system of government. It enables a society's self-determination through the mutual recognition of its members as equals under the law."[3] These fundamental freedoms grant self-determination through political participation—autonomy—on the one hand, and on the other hand they guarantee individual self-realization.

According to *The Economist*'s 2020 Democracy Index, there are 23 full democracies in the world. The Index also identifies 52 flawed democracies. In other words, out of 167 countries, just 75 can be regarded as democracies of any kind.[4] This means that over a third of the world's population lives under authoritarian regimes in which political freedom and freedom of speech are not protected. The pandemic has highlighted what it means when freedoms are restricted and the extent to which states, particularly authoritarian states, are able to do so—especially when other values are in danger. The pandemic puts health and lives at risk. Civil liberties were infringed in order to protect them—because freedom is a fundamental good that can only be experienced in a context and exists in a state of tension with other values. This context is constantly changing. If the state infringes fundamental rights, these infringements must be proportionate, because the core of fundamental rights is inviolable. This principle of proportionality is derived from the principle of justice.

The balancing of different values has varied over the course of history. Today we are increasingly seeing changes in society's understanding of the relationships in which freedom is possible.

Our view of freedom varies not just historically; different cultures also have different approaches to the concept. Take China for example. The Chinese government would argue that China too is a free country, because lived freedom (as opposed to theoretical freedom) is always a compromise that results from prioritizing different values. In the Chinese view, order and the common good take priority over political competition and individual freedoms in the hierarchy of values. There is nothing uniquely Chinese or oriental about this choice. Rather, Europe should ask itself whether it is not too self-assured when it comes to freedom. Challenges such as the escalating conflicts with authoritarian states threaten the Western concept of freedom, and digitalization, climate change, and pandemics can also change our views as freedom is in practice.

Let me take a closer look at the importance of freedom for human beings.

The philosopher Jean-Jacques Rousseau considered that the freedom of the individual, in addition to the choice between action and inaction, lies in the possibility of being able to start afresh—the new beginning as an expression and opportunity of the free person. In the 20th century, Hannah Arendt referred to this: for her, freedom lies in initiating and in being able to get started. It is through this ability to start anew and thus make a decision that the individual defines themselves. The individual is guided by their inner "daemon." This daemon is an internal compass that people follow when planning their lives. In philosophy, the concept of the daemon has been familiar since Socrates as an inner *telos* or law. In 1922 Max Weber wrote that we should "go about our work and meet the 'challenges of the day'—both in our human relations and in our vocation. But that moral is simple and straightforward if each person finds and obeys the daemon that holds the thread of *his* life."[5] This completes the circle. Freedom to act and start over, to follow your daemon and to define and differentiate yourself is a fundamental principle of being human. But of course, the place of freedom in the hierarchy of values changes throughout history.

The change in the understanding of freedom over the centuries is clearly reflected in literature. Goethe's concept of freedom tends towards activity, physical scope, and self-effectiveness. All this is embodied in the figure of Götz von Berlichingen. Everything he does is based on the maxim that people are free and must remain independent. Götz's last words in prison are "Freedom! Freedom!"[6] This view has changed over the centuries. Freedom is freedom from external constraints (negative freedom) and freedom to realize oneself (positive freedom).

The combination of positive and negative civil liberties shapes how we want to live together as a society today, because freedom is not a natural given but rather results from the interplay of socialization and constraints. Rules and laws are needed to maintain freedom, to guarantee it permanently, and to shape it. Freedom and order belong together; they are not opposites, because absolute freedom results in arbitrariness and a reign of terror and ultimately leads to chaos. One example that thinker Bazon Brock likes to cite is road traffic. "Only if I, like hopefully all other road users, obey the rules of the road strictly, can I move freely in traffic."[7] Freedom is only possible

through order. Order is the mother of freedom. This raises several questions:
- What are the limits of freedom?
- Is freedom consistent with values such as equality and social responsibility, or does freedom exist at the expense of these values?
- Can and should the state restrict freedoms to benefit the common good or national security, or to protect me from myself?
- How much responsibility does freedom entail?
- And is there a civil duty to use the freedom we have been given?

Such questions are as old as the idea of freedom itself. Freedom and equality; freedom and justice. These pairs of terms that were clearly defined in the context of liberalism are today becoming increasingly blurred. Are we seeing a shift in the scale of values in favor of equality and justice at the expense of freedom, a shift that is leading to a different understanding of freedom today?

My freedom ends where the freedom of others begins. The freedom of one generation ends where it begins to burden the next. As a result of climate change, for the first time a temporal perspective in the exercise of freedoms is involved, because a life based on freedom and led in a healthy environment is a core value that needs to be protected. Intertemporal responsibility is key,[8] not only with regard to future generations, but also with regard to weaker nations.

We are seeing new expressions of freedom—new ways of living in freedom. In 1958 the political philosopher and historian of ideas Isaiah Berlin concluded that there cannot be a world in which people are both free and equal.[9] A choice has to be made. The realization of one necessarily means a limitation of the other. Surveys carried out by the Allensbach Institute show that the prioritization of freedom or equality among German citizens is constantly changing. At the time of German reunification in 1990, freedom dominated with 60 percent. Freedom then declined in value, with the result that by 1997 a narrow majority voted in favor of equality.[10] In the years that followed, up to 2017, freedom was again prioritized. But even here there were exceptions: in 2006, 50 percent voted for equality and only 41 percent for freedom. In 2016 the result was 50-50; in 2017 freedom was once again in the lead by 10 percent.[11]

The choice will be fundamentally different for every individual, and this leads to the notion of pluralism. For Isaiah Berlin, the pluralism of values is fundamental to liberalism. But Berlin also reminds us that freedom must always be given special priority, because freedom alone enables people to realize other values and to achieve their own recognition. In practice, pluralism does not describe a society of individuals but a society composed of groups. It is important for any group to be recognized. Isaiah Berlin speaks of "recognition," i.e. belonging to a group and being recognized as a group.[12]

Our society is taking this route if we think of the LGBTQ community, for example, or the opening up of society to people who are not "white and male." Increasingly, individual groups stand side by side on an equal footing. This is where the concept of "equaliberty" becomes relevant. Increasingly, freedom and equality are seen as two sides of the same coin. For the French philosopher Étienne Balibar, freedom and equality enjoy the same conditions: both values are "expressions of the communitarian being of men [and] institutions" and presuppose each other.[13] There needs to be a balance between communality (equality) and individuality (freedom). Increases in diversity enable greater personal development and thus an increase in freedom. However, this also goes hand in hand with a growing demand on the individual to behave in a way that recognizes and tolerates others—i.e. to restrain themselves under certain circumstances too. This results in a tension between gains in freedom and increases in consideration or self-restraint for the benefit of the common good. This not only affects the way we live in society alongside other people, but also our relationship with other living creatures and the natural world. Underpinning this is a new understanding of being human—as one who no longer sees themselves as the pinnacle of creation, but as part of it, and who can and wants to live freely only by coexisting with people, animals, and plants.

This means we need a shift in perspective and paradigm. And if we're lucky, we can see this already happening. In her book *Les Lumières à l'âge du vivant*, the French philosopher Corine Pelluchon talks about a "new Enlightenment."[14] In the Convoco podcast she says: "A new Enlightenment requires profound changes in our self-image and our coexistence. I already see the harbingers of such an age. Many people care about animals and interest in ecology is growing, especially among the younger generation. This development could transform ecological changes into a movement of emancipation."[15] It is about creating the kind of insight that is based on appreciating others. Freedom in this century means increased recognition of the individual while at the same time being more considerate: freedom not as egoism, but as a combination of appreciation, consideration, and self-restraint through insight. We need to take a long-term perspective to deal with today's challenges. The goal must be living in a healthy world. In order to achieve this goal, it is important to forgo the freedom of short-term gains in pleasure.

These are the reasons why we are devoting ourselves to the topic of freedom, and why we have chosen an apparent paradox as the title—how much freedom must we forgo to be free? We are all aware that we need to change our behavior. But is it really losing freedom if we achieve a greater good in exchange?

Corinne Michaela Flick, January 2022

Notes

1. CONVOCO! Survey on Freedom, July 25, 2021, https://www.convoco.co.uk/convoco-survey-on-freedom/ (accessed December 22, 2021).

2. Paul Kirchhof, "Freedom in the Crisis" in Corinne Michaela Flick (ed.), *Can't Pay, Won't Pay? Sovereign Debt and the Challenge of Growth in Europe* (Munich: Convoco Editions, 2013), pp. 89–90.

3. Stefan Korioth, "Autonomy and Protection—Ambivalences in Fundamental Rights" in the present volume, pp. 109–123.

4. Economist Intelligence Unit, "Democracy Index 2020: In Sickness and in Health?" EIU 2021, p. 3.

5. Max Weber, *Science as a Vocation*, trans. Rodney Livingstone (Indianapolis/Cambridge: Hackett Publishing Company, 2004), p. 31, https://hscif.org/wp-content/uploads/2018/04/Max-Weber-Science-as-a-Vocation.pdf (accessed February 3, 2022).

6. Johann Wolfgang Goethe, *Götz von Berlichingen* (New York: F. Ungar Publishing Company, 1965), p. 130.

7. Bazon Brock, "Freiheit – Das Pathos der Ordnungen," January 1990 (newspaper article).

8. Referring to "intertemporal guarantees of freedom," Germany's Federal Constitutional Court declared parts of the Federal Climate Protection Act to be unconstitutional in a decision on March 24, 2021, since a large part of the necessary emission reductions were postponed to the future at the expense of future generations: "As intertemporal guarantees of freedom, fundamental rights afford the complainants protection against comprehensive threats to freedom caused by the greenhouse gas reduction burdens that are mandatory under Art. 20a GG being unilaterally offloaded onto the future." The Federal Constitutional Court, Press Release no. 31/2021, April 29, 2021, https://www.bundesverfassungsgericht.de/SharedDocs/Pressemitteilungen/EN/2021/bvg21-031.html (accessed November 11, 2022).

9. "The world that we encounter in ordinary experience is one in which we are faced with choices between ends equally ultimate, and claims equally absolute, the realization of some of which must inevitable involve the sacrifice of others" in Isaiah Berlin, "Two Concepts of Liberty" in *Four Essays on Liberty*, ed. Isaiah Berlin (Oxford: Oxford University Press, 1969), p. 28.

10. Institut für Demoskopie Allensbach, *Der Wert der Freiheit*, October/November 2003, p. 57.

11. John Stuart Mill Institut und Institut für Demoskopie Allensbach, Ergebnisdossier Freiheitsindex 2017, Wie halten es die Deutschen mit der Freheit? Schwerpunkt "Populistische Herausforderungen der Demokratie," 2017, p. 14.

12. Berlin "Two Concepts of Liberty," pp. 21–25.

13. Étienne Balibar, *Equaliberty: Political Essays*, trans. James Ingram (Durham NC: Duke University Press, 2014), p. 55.

14. Corine Pelluchon, *Les Lumières à l'âge du vivant* (Paris: Seuil, 2021).

15. Corine Pelluchon and Corinne Flick, "Why we have to overcome the dualism between nature and culture," CONVOCO! Podcast (51), August 2021, https://www.convoco.co.uk/podcast/51-corine-pelluchon-why-we-have-to-overcome-the-dualism-between-nature-and-culture-2 (accessed October 13, 2021).

THESES

TIMO MEYNHARDT

In a world full of contradictions and conflicts, the internal freedom gained through self-reflection is more important than abstract declarations of freedom. The way to more external freedom is via greater internal freedom.

CLAUDIA WIESNER

Representative democracy must combine freedom and equality in equal value and in relation to each other. The self-government of the democratic sovereign is based on these principles, which are implemented through institutions, processes, and rights. Freedom and equality are not only mutually dependent, but also mutually restrictive.

CLEMENS FUEST

In a country where a dangerous virus is rampant, the economy cannot flourish. That is why effective pandemic control is a prerequisite for positive economic development. There is no conflict between protecting health and protecting the economy.

BRUNO KAHL

Freedom and security are by no means opposites that can be played off against one another—they are mutually dependent.

BAZON BROCK

Those who advance a choice between order or freedom destroy both and are not in any way establishing a higher law, whether nationalist or divine.

RUDOLF MELLINGHOFF

The principle of the tax state and tax limits based on basic rights characterize the financing of the state based on civil liberties. They form the foundations of a free, democratic constitutional state which, on the one hand, guarantees social security and freedom through state services and, at the same time, respects the free system of labor and capital as well as property remaining in the hands of private individuals.

HILDEGARD WORTMANN

Personal mobility means freedom, self-determination, and independence. The task now is to make personal mobility sustainable. We need effective cooperation between politics, business, and society to develop solutions that give people the freedom to live sustainably and that contribute to a better life. If that succeeds, sustainability does not mean forgoing anything. Sustainability is the new premium.

MONIKA SCHNITZER

Competition forces companies to compete for their customers through affordable prices, good services, new ideas, and better products. Competition increases people's economic freedom by increasing their choice.

GABRIEL FELBERMAYR

In order to ensure the stability of the world trade system, the EU needs new defensive instruments. But it is important not to lose sight of the goal of open markets, otherwise the EU, together with its trading partners, may find itself in a zero-sum game in which economic freedoms are shrinking on all sides.

HANS ULRICH OBRIST

As the Oulipian writer Harry Mathews once told me, freedom can sometimes lie in constraints: by changing the rules of the game, one can find new freedom within these rules. To ask "How much freedom must we forgo to be free?" is therefore to ask how we can reconsider what we forgo not as a loss, but as an opportunity to create.

MARTHA JUNGWIRTH

I want to put something on canvas or on paper that is open-ended so that everyone who looks at it—including myself—can make something new from it. So nothing is fixed, nothing controlled.

PHILIPP PATTBERG

In order to leave behind wasteful lifestyles and business cycles, fossil fuels, and a murderous food regime, we need to ensure a big integrative meta-narrative, international solidarity and focus on the silent, reasonable majority. Under these conditions, freedom and a stable climate are not a contradiction.

PETER WITTIG

The new superpower rivalry between the US and China is Europe's greatest challenge. China is becoming a litmus test of transatlantic relations as well. European equidistance between both superpowers is not an option. Instead, the EU needs a joint China agenda with the US that describes a differentiated relationship: China as a partner, a competitor, and (on certain issues) an adversary.

SVEN SIMON

In order to defend the European model of freedom, Europeans must assume the power to act. This requires a paradigm shift from internal to global orientation, and, to legitimize this, we need a real competition of opinions at European level, a shared public sphere, and a focus on those issues where European cooperation brings concrete and visible added value.

HERBERT A. REITSAMER

The findings of neuroscience and philosophy cannot question the laws of physics. Within the framework of natural laws and the enormous complexity of our brain, the scope and possibility for free decisions and ultimately free will can arise.

TIM CRANE

One danger of restricting freedom of speech is that it can also restrict freedom of thought. A liberal state can of course legitimately prohibit certain forms of speech if they genuinely cause harm. But the state cannot and should not compel belief.

STEFAN KORIOTH

Fundamental rights protect freedom, i.e. the ability of the individual to choose between different courses of action and to take responsibility for the consequences of their own decisions. There are two approaches to this: the aim of the classical approach is to leave the individual unchallenged in their own development. The new approach requires the state to create and protect the prerequisites for the exercise of freedom. The two approaches can be conflicting.

CORINNE MICHAELA FLICK

Freedom in this century means increased recognition of the individual while at the same time being more considerate: freedom not as egotism, but as a combination of mutual appreciation and self-restraint through insight. It is important to take a long-term perspective.

JÖRN LEONHARD

A look back at the 19th century shows us not merely the range of various notions of freedom. Above all, it points out that the definition of freedom has always included polarity and being interwoven with other value concepts. The latter formed and still form the basis of how concepts of freedom develop, how they are challenged, adapted, and redefined.

BIRKE HÄCKER

The idea of "freedom" (or "liberty") is a powerful and at the same time highly complex postulate. It is centered around the individual, yet always in a larger societal context. In order to understand how it is possible to be "free" by forgoing freedom, we must distinguish the "positive" and "negative" concepts of liberty and take a closer look at freedom's individual and social dimensions.

CHAPTER 1

THE ECONOMIC CONSEQUENCES OF RESTRICTING FREEDOMS DURING THE COVID-19 PANDEMIC

CLEMENS FUEST

1. INTRODUCTION: IS THERE A CONFLICT BETWEEN HEALTH, CIVIL LIBERTIES, AND THE ECONOMY?

In the debate about the management of the COVID-19 pandemic, the economic consequences of government measures to contain infection are a central concern. The economic impact is closely related to the consequences these measures have on individual freedoms, but they are nevertheless different. Prohibiting people from leaving the house to take a walk in the evening, to visit a museum, or to meet friends is a serious infringement of civil liberties. Economic costs are usually not associated with this, at least in public debates, although such costs do arise, as will be explained below.

In public debates in Germany and many other countries, state-imposed restrictions on social contact with the aim of curbing the spread of COVID-19 were often seen as imposing a heavy burden on economic development. It was argued that there is a conflict between protecting health and protecting the economy. Time and again, demands were made to relax social contact restrictions or not impose them in the first place in order to prevent economic damage. In fact, the idea that not imposing restrictions on social contact and accepting higher numbers of infections would help prevent economic damage is misleading. This essay explains why this is the case and will also discuss other lessons emerging from the crisis regarding the economic aspects of government pandemic management.

2. THE ECONOMIC COSTS OF PANDEMICS

Pandemics are momentous events in human history. The most significant costs of pandemics are the great loss of human life and the damage incurred to the health of many survivors. But pandemics also have far-reaching economic consequences. Epidemics of the plague that affected Europe in the 14th century in particular cost many lives. As a result, labor became scarce in lots of countries and economic output fell significantly.

The global influenza pandemic that struck in 1918 and is still unfairly referred to as "Spanish flu,"[1] is estimated to have killed 40 million people between 1918 and 1920. It had a serious economic impact. There were three waves to the pandemic. It broke out in the spring of 1918, probably in Haskell County, Kansas. This is a rural area of the United States which was unfortunately the location of a large training camp for soldiers who were preparing for their deployment in World War I— in Europe in particular. When the soldiers were dispatched, the influenza spread first in the US, then in the trenches of the European battlefields, and ultimately worldwide. Between September 1918 and February 1919, a second and particularly deadly wave of infections took hold. A third wave of infections followed in the course of 1919.

The consequences for the war-torn economy were devastating. A study of economic history concludes that economic output in the countries affected plummeted by 6 to 8 percent.[2] Since the pandemic coincided with the end of World War I, it is not easy to measure the economic impact, but it is undeniable that the losses were huge. Interestingly, the effects of today's COVID-19 pandemic are creating a similar-sized loss of growth, although economic circumstances have changed significantly over the past hundred years.

Over the past few decades, local epidemics have emerged time and again: for example, the SARS epidemic that broke out in China in 2003. The SARS virus claimed 8,000 lives in 37 countries, so the impact was not comparable to that of the influenza pandemic after World War I or the COVID-19 pandemic. The economic consequences were correspondingly smaller and, according to estimates, entailed no more than a decline in growth of around 1 percent of China's economic output.

The COVID-19 pandemic is not yet over, but it is already evident that it has incurred considerable costs in the shape of lost economic output. Before the pandemic, for example, Germany's economic growth in 2020 was expected to be just over 1 percent; in the event, gross domestic product shrank by 5 percent due to the crisis. The loss of growth, i.e. the difference between the expected scenario without a crisis and the growth that actually occurred, amounts to more than 6 percent of gross domestic product. Some countries had to deal with even stronger slowdowns in growth. In 2020 GDP shrank by 10.8 percent in Spain, in the UK the decline was 9.8 percent, in Italy 8.9 percent, and in France 8 percent. Worldwide the recession caused by COVID-19 has greatly exceeded the global financial crisis of 2008/09, bringing about the worst economic crisis since the traumatic global depression of the 1930s.[3]

However, it would not be appropriate to equate the economic costs of pandemics with the effects on growth of gross domestic product. There are several reasons for this. First, medical expenditure on drugs, masks, and patient care are among the costs of the pandemic, but the production of such goods and health services increases gross domestic product. The costs are entailed in that, without the pandemic, the resources they use up could have been employed for other purposes, such as treating other illnesses that were often neglected during the pandemic.

Second, the decline in gross domestic product does not include the loss of schooling and vocational training. In this instance, costs in the form of reduced productivity due to missed training and education will only become apparent in the future. Third, during the pandemic, companies and employees had to be supported using a substantial amount of public funds. In the short term this was financed by increasing the national debt. In the medium term, however, higher taxes will have to be levied or government spending cut in order to service the debt. Higher taxes or the cancellation of government spending, especially reductions in public investment, could have a negative impact on future economic development.

Fourth, the pandemic entails costs in the form of a lack of social life, which is of great importance for the quality of many people's lives, but it is not recognized as an element of gross domestic product. If people do not visit friends and relatives, or engage in community life and shared activities, this causes high stress levels that may damage physical and mental health—these too are indeed costs in the economic sense. In order to measure the extent of these costs, we would have to determine how much those affected would be willing to pay to eliminate hypothetically the risk of contagion caused by the pandemic. The sums of money would undoubtedly be considerable.

3. THE ECONOMIC COSTS AND PROFITS RESULTING FROM MEASURES TAKEN TO CONTAIN PANDEMICS

The fact that the COVID-19 pandemic has entailed high economic costs and damaged health, and that these factors cannot be reduced to the production losses recognized as part of gross domestic product, is unlikely to be controversial.[4] What is controversial, by contrast, is the effect government social contact restrictions imposed to contain the pandemic have on economic development. As mentioned earlier, there is a widespread perception that there is a conflict between protecting health on the one hand and protecting the economy on the other. At first glance, this seems plausible. On closer inspection, however, it turns out that this idea is misleading. The most crucial mistake is not differentiating sufficiently between the effects of government social contact restrictions and the effects of the pandemic itself.

To illustrate this it is helpful to consider the basic economic effects of pandemics and government social contact restrictions. In principle, it is possible that a government-ordered shut-down of economic activities would entail economic costs. If a restaurant that without government intervention would be full or at least well patronized is not allowed to open, prosperity-creating economic activity disappears. However, we should bear in mind that restaurant patrons who are afraid of being infected with a dangerous virus are less likely to go to the restaurant and are more likely to stay at home. During the COVID-19 pandemic, this applies above all to older people, who generally spend more money in restaurants than younger people, but who are at considerably greater risk from the virus. Therefore, we cannot assume that without government social contact restrictions restaurants would have been anywhere near as full as prior to the pandemic. Part of the damage is thus caused by the pandemic itself, not by government social contact restrictions.[5] Measuring the proportion of the damage caused by the pandemic itself is an empirical question.

Extensive research has now been done on this subject, but it mainly relates to the earlier phase of the pandemic, essentially to experiences and data from 2020. The idea that one could limit the economic damage of a dangerous pandemic by dispensing with government social contact restrictions and accept the spread of the pathogen is refuted by the available empirical literature on the economic effects of the pandemic. There are two main issues involved. First, such a policy prolongs and exacerbates waves of infection. Second, as already mentioned, people react to the risk of becoming infected independently of government measures by refraining from certain types of consumption. This is especially true of high-income older people, whose spending is very important for economic development. This is shown, for example, by studies that compare consumer behavior in US states that have a variety of lockdown policies. US states that locked down later or that re-opened the economy earlier as compared to states with similar rates of infection, show no significantly higher level of social consumption, i.e. visits to restaurants, hairdressers, or events.[6]

An example of an empirical study that documents these relationships in great detail is the study by Goolsbee and Syverson.[7] Their study uses cellphone data to examine whether customers in US states without lockdown measures visit stores more often than in states where such visits are sometimes not even possible because many stores have been obliged to close. The authors analyze customer visits in 2.25 million retail and service companies in 110 different sectors, in each case comparing customers who live in the same region but are subject to different lockdown measures because the region is divided by a county line or a US state border. The result is unequivocal: in the pandemic in spring 2020, businesses lost an average of 60 percent of their customers, with government lockdown measures accounting for just 7 of these percentage points. With the same infection rate, but without government lockdown measures, the decline in economic activity was almost 90 percent of that observed in regions that imposed lockdown measures.

In Europe, Sweden pursued its own path in the early phase of the pandemic and initially waived lockdown measures. Comparisons of labor market developments in Sweden with other Scandinavian countries show that the crisis-related decline in employment in Sweden emerged a little later and was a little less pronounced than in neighboring countries that had implemented lockdown measures earlier. Nevertheless, the loss of employment was in the end around 80 percent of the loss of employment in countries with lockdown measures.[8] In addition, in 2020 Sweden suffered a similar drop in growth to other Scandinavian countries, but significantly more deaths—as much as around ten times as many as Norway.

The overall picture provided by the available empirical evidence suggests that at least 80 percent of the costs in the form of lack of added value in the area of social consumption are caused by the presence of the virus and the risk of contagion itself, not by government lockdown measures.

One could argue that lockdown measures are unnecessary if people voluntarily avoid contact. It is true that government regulations restricting social contacts are often less binding than one might think if one doesn't take account of the fact that in a pandemic situation people avoid the risk of contagion anyway. But to demand that state-imposed social contact restrictions be dispensed with entirely would be a step too far. There certainly exist groups who are not prepared to restrict their social contacts and who accept the risk of infection. In the COVID-19 pandemic, health risks correlate strongly with age. Young people in particular are less at risk from the disease, which is why the "voluntary" avoidance of social contact is less pronounced among this cohort. That would be acceptable if the risk of infection and other costs only applied to those who consciously take the risk of becoming infected. However, this is not the case because this behavior increases the spread of the virus considerably.

From an economic perspective, we can see a classic problem of external effects here. In making decisions, individuals take into account the risk to their own health but not the consequences for others. In this instance, the consequences are not only that the risk of infection increases for others, but also that people who take risks put a strain on the publicly funded health system, which is reaching the limits of full capacity in the pandemic. In this context, to be fair, it should be noted that there are also other areas in which risks incurred by the behavior of individuals are passed on to the general public via the health system—we might think of leisure activities such as skiing that are likely to cause injury. However, it does not follow from this that such behavior is to be tolerated, but rather that measures such as higher health-insurance premiums for skiers would make sense.

There is considerable evidence to show that state-imposed restrictions on social contacts contain infections, although they are not binding for many people. This is not only because certain groups are unwilling to voluntarily restrict their social contacts; some groups cannot do this at all, for example children who are subject to compulsory education and have to go to school unless state regulations abolish compulsory education or ensure that lessons can take place online.

Government measures to reduce infections are not only able to restrict the amount of economic damage. To the extent that they contain and shorten waves of infection and thus enable social consumption to open up again earlier, they can even reduce the economic costs of the pandemic. However, this does not apply to policies introducing restrictions that operate in such a way that infections tend to remain constant rather than decrease. A "lockdown light" that does not actually lead to a reduction in the number of infections can be extremely ineffective.[9] In such a lockdown, it's possible that introducing tighter measures will not put a strain on the economy, but rather protect it because it shortens the duration of the measures.

However, all this does not mean that lockdown measures of any kind are unproblematic for the economy. In the first weeks and months of the pandemic, national borders were closed not just to private travelers and businesspeople, but also in many cases to the transport of goods. The latter has hardly helped contain the pandemic. However, the disruption to goods traffic has led to a collapse in industrial production. Raw materials and intermediate products were no longer delivered and cross-border value chains interrupted, resulting in a considerable loss of production and short-time working in sectors with sometimes very high added value.

As the pandemic continued, it was possible to lift border closures and ease other obstacles to freight traffic. This has enabled global industry to recover remarkably quickly. Occasionally, however, disruptions still occur. Over the course of the year, for example, delivery problems for industrial raw materials and intermediate goods increased again, partly due to unexpectedly strong demand, but also in part because logistics facilities such as ports were affected repeatedly by shutdowns caused by the pandemic.

4. RESTRICTING SOCIAL CONTACTS ALONE IS NOT ENOUGH

We may accept that using lockdown measures among other things to protect public health during the pandemic does not conflict with protecting the economy, but it does not follow that it makes sense or is acceptable for government pandemic management to be limited to lockdown measures. A policy that is limited to imposing social contact restrictions curtails freedoms more than necessary and fails to avert economic damage. Pandemic management in Germany and many other countries was particularly weak in this regard. What would have been required was more proactive measures beyond restricting social contact, above all more testing and faster track-and-trace of infections. On the one hand, this would have significantly reduced the spread of the virus, and on the other, social and economic life could have opened up earlier as a result of more testing and hygiene measures.

The failures in education are particularly apparent. Current economic studies of education conclude that missing one third of a year of schooling can reduce the lifetime income of children and young people by up to 4 percent. During the pandemic, some lessons were moved online, but not all schools were able to do this quickly, mainly because of a lack of technical and organizational infrastructure. In addition, online schooling cannot really replace face-to-face teaching. This is especially true for children from families in which the parents cannot help with learning, especially in less educated settings. A policy that is limited to lockdown measures and does not fight the pandemic proactively through extensive testing and tracing of infections increases not only the damage to health but also the economic costs of the pandemic.

5. MACROECONOMIC STABILIZATION POLICIES

As already mentioned, the pandemic is also having a significant impact on public finances. The national debt has risen significantly. Over the coming years, servicing these debts means a burden on economic development and a loss of freedoms, insofar as higher taxes and a decline in public services can restrict the individual's scope for freedom. Nevertheless, another important lesson from the crisis is that decisive action to stabilize the economy and support employees and the self-employed in the sectors affected has prevented a worse outcome. Targeted measures were essential, however. Classical instruments of economic policy aimed at supporting overall economic demand were less appropriate. Ultimately, in a pandemic situation the problem is not that there is insufficient purchasing power, it is that economic activity that involves people mixing together and causing a risk of infection is impossible. Macroeconomic stabilization policies therefore had to concentrate primarily on providing a bridge during the pandemic period. The aim was to ensure that as little irreparable damage as possible occurs during this time. It was also about stabilizing the financial markets, where in particular there is a growing risk during crises that confidence will decline and banks will stop lending money to companies and private households. That can easily lead to a self-perpetuating, worsening crisis. The government can prevent such a development by providing state loans, guarantees, and equity aid, alongside the support of the central bank.

One of the long-term consequences of these interventions is that many companies have been saved from closure or bankruptcy. Critics point out that this also provides support for companies whose business model is not sustainable in the long term. That is certainly true. Structural change is important for economic development, even if it can be painful for people who are involved in companies that are downsizing or threatened with bankruptcy. However, it is questionable whether structural change can happen during an extreme economic crisis. In crises it therefore seems reasonable to accept that among the companies receiving support there are also some that will turn out to be unsustainable in the long term. Overall, there is much to suggest that the economic slump caused by the pandemic would have been much deeper without the implementation of macroeconomic stabilization measures.

6. CONCLUSION AND OUTLOOK

Over the course of the COVID-19 pandemic, the governments in many countries intervened far more intensively in individual freedoms than many people had experienced in previous crises or emergencies. To a large extent this also applied to economic freedoms. In debates about pandemic management, it has been claimed time and again that restricting social contacts with the aim of protecting against infection placed a heavy burden on economic development. In this respect, it is claimed, there is a conflict between protecting health and protecting the economy. This view is misleading and does not accurately reflect the complexity of the crisis. In a country where a dangerous virus is rampant, the economy cannot flourish. That is why effective pandemic control is a prerequisite for positive economic development. This does not mean that any kind of social contact restriction is justified, and certainly not that pandemic management can be limited to restricting social contacts. An important lesson from the COVID-19 pandemic is that, for example, more testing and faster tracing of cases of infection are fundamental to combating a pandemic successfully. Economic recovery and the regaining and protection of individual freedoms require proactive and targeted action by politics, business, and society.

Notes

1. Spain was neutral during the war and press censorship did not prevent media coverage, so initially Spain alone was reporting openly about the pandemic. As a result, it was initially thought that the influenza originated in Spain.
2. Robert Barro, José F. Ursúa, and Joanna Weng, "The Coronavirus and the Great Influenza Pandemic: Lessons from the 'Spanish Flu' for the Coronavirus's Potential Effects on Mortality and Economic Activity" in National Bureau of Economic Research (NBER), Working Paper 26866, 2020.
3. Clemens Fuest, *Wie wir unsere Wirtschaft retten: Der Weg aus der Corona-Krise* (Berlin: Aufbau-Verlag, 2020).
4. On this subject, see also Florian Dorn et al., "Die volkswirtschaftlichen Kosten des Corona-Shutdown für Deutschland: Eine Szenarienrechnung," in ifo Schnelldienst 2020, 73, no. 04, pp. 29–35.
5. Andrea Abele-Brehm et al., "Die Bekämpfung der Coronavirus-Pandemie tragfähig gestalten. Empfehlungen für eine flexible, risikoadaptierte Strategie," unpublished manuscript, 2020.
6. Raj Chetty et al., "The Economic Impacts of COVID-19: Evidence from a New Public Database Built Using Private Sector Data," in NBER, Working Paper 27431, 2020.
7. Austan Goolsbee and Chad Syverson, "Fear, Lockdown, and Diversion: Comparing Drivers of Pandemic Economic Decline 2020," in NBER, Working Paper 27432, 2020.

8. Steffen Juranek et al., "Labor Market Effects of Covid-19 in Sweden and Its Neighbors: Evidence from Novel Administrative Data," in CESifo, Working Paper 8473, 2020.

9. Florian Dorn et al., "In the Common Interest of Health and Economy: A Scenario Calculation for Containing the Coronavirus Pandemic," in ifo Schnelldienst 2020, 1, no. 06, pp. 1–9.

CHAPTER 2

COMPETITION AS A GUARANTOR OF FREEDOM

MONIKA SCHNITZER

In summer 2021, on July 9, US President Joe Biden signed an executive order instructing the government to work towards creating more competition.[1] He handed over the pen with which he signed the executive order to Lina Khan, the new head of the Federal Trade Commission, the US competition authority. Alongside Lina Khan, Joe Biden also appointed Tim Wu as a new member of the National Economic Council and Jonathan Kanter as the new head of the Antitrust Division in the Department of Justice. With these three nominations, the President has sent a clear signal that his term of office will focus on strengthening competition, because all three are proven critics of the growth of monopolies, especially in the shape of the big-tech companies. In his speech, Biden emphasized the importance of open and fair competition as a basis on which capitalism can lead to prosperity and growth, saying, "Capitalism without competition isn't capitalism, it's exploitation."[2] And he went on to say that competition forces companies to compete for their customers through affordable prices, good services, new ideas, and better products. As I would put it, competition increases people's economic freedom by increasing their choice.

The ways in which a lack of competition limits economic freedoms is illustrated by the examples that Biden himself mentions in his speech. One fifth of the US population, according to one of these examples, has access to just one Internet provider and therefore pays on average five times as much as other people who have a choice of different providers. Not having freedom of choice means paying inflated prices.

A second example concerns the freedom of choice for employees. One in three US companies requires its employees to sign so-called "non-compete" clauses. These are clauses that prohibit employees from going to work for competing businesses, and that may be justified in the case of highly qualified employees, as they prevent them from passing on trade secrets to the competition. In the US, however, they are often demanded of employees in considerably lower skilled occupations, such as construction workers, hotel employees, or employees in fast-food restaurants. Anyone who signs such a non-compete clause is considerably limited in their own freedom to choose a new employer. Therefore, with his executive order, Biden wants, among other things, to prohibit or restrict the use of such clauses.

With this call for more competition, President Biden sees himself following the tradition of the two Roosevelts: Theodore Roosevelt, who broke up large trusts such as Standard Oil in the first decade of the 20th century, and Franklin D. Roosevelt, who in the 1930s brought dozens of antitrust proceedings against the increasing monopolization of the economy.

In reality, the concept of competition as a guarantor of freedom was and is by no means a sure-fire success. Let's take a look back at the early days of antitrust legislation in the United States. In 1890 the so-called Sherman Act was passed, the first antitrust law in the United States. It was a reaction against the increasing monopolization that was taking place in the late 19th century, against the creation of so-called trusts, hence the name, "antitrust."[3] Section 2 of the Sherman Act states: "Every person who shall monopolize, or attempt to monopolize ... any part of the trade or commerce among the several States, or with foreign nations, shall be deemed guilty of a felony."

In the first decade after the law was passed, however, it was not really used as intended. Five years after the Sherman Act was signed, the Supreme Court cleared the way for mergers that gave American Sugar a 98 percent share of the market. Instead, federal courts used the Sherman Act to prevent trade unions from merging to form larger entities.[4]

Concentration in the corporate sector continued to increase. Around the turn of the century, practically every major industry was controlled by a monopoly—trusts such as Standard Oil, US Steel, trusts in the railway sector, as well as the AT&T monopoly in the telecommunications sector. A Tobacco Trust, a Cotton Trust, a Sugar Trust, a Rubber Trust, a Filmmaker Trust, trusts in the sectors manufacturing watches, nails etc., were all set up. The founders of these trusts themselves saw nothing bad in this, as they saw themselves as building a new and better society.[5] For them, monopolies were a superior form of economic organization that prevented ruinous competition, to which many companies at the end of the 19th century, so they believed, had been sacrificed.

The Sherman Act was only implemented in the way intended by the legislators under Theodore Roosevelt. Following the laissez-faire policy of his predecessor, McKinley, he took the view that it was the point of antitrust laws to ensure that in a democracy the elected representatives, not the "corporate bosses," had the last word.

So Theodore Roosevelt initiated dozens of antitrust proceedings, culminating in a series of breakups, the most famous of these being the aforementioned breakup of Standard Oil under Roosevelt's successor, President William H. Taft. President Wilson, Taft's successor, tightened competition rules through the 1914 Clayton Act and set up the Federal Trade Commission to enforce these rules.

In the 1930s, as a result of the Great Depression, business concentration increased again. President Franklin D. Roosevelt watched this with alarm, as he saw that this endangered not only the people's economic freedom but also their political freedom. A speech he gave in Congress in 1938 began by stating: "... the liberty of a democracy is not safe if the people tolerate the growth of private power to a point where it becomes stronger than their democratic state itself."[6]

In his State of the Union address in 1944, Roosevelt also emphasized: "True individual freedom cannot exist without economic security and independence." That is why Franklin D. Roosevelt called for a second Bill of Rights, which should guarantee, among other things: "the right of every businessman, large and small, to trade in an atmosphere of freedom from unfair competition and domination by monopolies at home or abroad."[7] Guided by this belief, the number of antitrust proceedings under Franklin D. Roosevelt's presidency multiplied in the years that followed.

Concern about antitrust proceedings alone had a remarkable disciplinary effect on companies. One example of this is the antitrust proceedings against AT&T, which began in 1949. According to those familiar with the case, this prompted AT&T to standardize the patents for the newly invented transistor and to license them at reasonable fees, as they wanted to avoid drawing the competition watchdogs' attention to AT&T's market power. As I have shown, writing with my co-authors, this licensing policy led to a major boom in innovation and thus significantly advanced the development of the computer.[8] However, AT&T was not broken up in this antitrust case, but only in the subsequent case against AT&T in 1984.

In the decades that followed, there were significantly fewer cases of successful antitrust proceedings. The case against IBM was dropped at the same time as the decision was taken to break up AT&T. The breakup of Microsoft, which had been initiated by the Department of Justice, was rejected by the court on appeal in 2001.

The reason for the reluctance of the competition authorities and the failure of the court cases may have been the growing influence of the Chicago School. Robert Bork, arguably the School's most prominent exponent, argued that market monopoly is not a problem *per se*. He said that it is not the task of antitrust law to protect competition as such. Rather, its only task is to ensure consumer welfare, which is expressed in the prices that consumers have to pay. In order to reject a merger, he continued, the competition authority must prove that such a merger would lead to price increases. Mergers should not be prohibited without evidence of such harm. In the eyes of the Chicago School, the concentration of economic power, which Franklin D. Roosevelt saw as a threat to democracy, does not pose a problem.

While in Europe too this line of argument became more widespread, European developments were somewhat different. With the establishment of the

European Union Single Market in 1989, the monitoring of mergers that are significant to more than one of the Member States was transferred to the EU's area of responsibility.[9] The European competition authority in the form of the Directorate-General for Competition, a part of the European Commission, was given great independence. Thomas Philippon attributes this to the competition between Member States. In his book *The Great Reversal* he interprets this as follows: "Each country wanted to be sure that other countries would not be able to influence the EU institutions to their advantage."[10] In Philippon's opinion, the European Union has benefited significantly from these stricter competition controls compared to the United States, an assessment that I agree with.

But European competition policy has also had a hard time finding an answer to increasing market concentration, especially in the area of the digital economy. The big-tech companies, the so-called GAFAMs (Google, Amazon, Facebook, Apple, Microsoft) are more or less dominant in their sector. Google dominates the search-engine market, Amazon dominates the online commerce market, Facebook dominates the social media market, and so on. As was the case 120 years ago, these monopolies too have grown not least through hundreds of corporate takeovers, including some that have turned out to be problematic not just in retrospect, such as Facebook's acquisition of WhatsApp and Instagram—problematic because at least some of them could have become potential competitors.

That the competition authorities allowed these mergers was due, among other things, to the fact that the acquired start-ups generated little or no turnover and were therefore below the relevant thresholds for mergers. In some cases too, misrepresentation has allayed competition authorities' concerns. For example, when buying WhatsApp, Facebook assured the authorities that the data from the two services would not be linked because this was technically impossible. In retrospect, however, this turned out to be untrue, and the data has been integrated all along. So in these markets we cannot really talk about functioning competition. That raises two questions:

1. Is competition in the traditional sense at all possible in the digital economy or is monopolization inevitable due to the particular characteristics of digital markets?

2. What does this dominance of the major big-tech companies mean for the freedom of their users?

Is there any kind of problem here? Don't these companies offer great products that many of us use enthusiastically and for which, at least at first glance, we don't even have to pay anything?

There are two main reasons why digital markets are dominated by a few companies: the specific characteristics of these digital markets on the one hand and the anti-competitive behavior of the major big-tech companies on the other.

What are the specific characteristics of these markets? Online markets are typically characterized by high economies of scale and network effects. This can be illustrated particularly well using the example of social media. Economists speak of economies of scale when larger quantities can be produced at lower unit costs than smaller quantities. This is the case when the fixed costs are high but the variable costs are low. Programming a platform like Facebook is very expensive, but its development incurs just a one-time cost, regardless of how many people are using the platform. That is why such an investment is all the more worthwhile the more users it has. Network effects arise when the benefit for the individual increases with the number of other people using the platform, because more friends can be contacted. Both effects, the economies of scale and the network effects, mean that such markets easily "tip," so that in the end only one provider remains, even if it does not necessarily offer the best service.

Equally, however, these markets become monopolies because the big-tech companies repeatedly use questionable, not to say anti-competitive practices in order to expand their market power and extend it to other markets. This can be illustrated well using the example of the Google search engine. For a long time, Google has made sure that its search engine is installed as the default on mobile phones. Most people don't bother actively installing and using another search engine when Google Search is so easy to access. The consequence of this, however, is that competing search-engine providers find it difficult to gain a foothold and expand in the search-engine market. As a result, Google now has a share of over 90 percent in the search-engine market, which in turn means that Google dominates the enormously profitable market for online advertising.[11]

How exactly does Google ensure it is the default search engine? In the case of Apple phones, Google pays to be installed by default. In all other cases, Google uses its control over Google Android, the only relevant operating system for mobile phones besides that of Apple, and its dominance over certain apps that customers absolutely want to have on their smartphones such as Google Playstore, to put pressure on manufacturers. The operating system and apps are only available if Google Search is installed as the standard search engine.[12] The EU Commission tried to prevent this behavior by imposing conditions in the proceedings against Google Android, but without any tangible success. Google has complied with the conditions to the letter but has *de facto* circumvented them by rewriting its contracts.[13] New search-engine providers such as the Munich start-up Cliqz had to throw in the towel.

So, one might object, what's the problem? Aren't the products of the big-tech companies just very good, don't the companies invest a lot in innovations, don't people voluntarily choose to use these services, which they also get free of charge? I cannot answer all these questions with an unreserved yes.

Are the products really that good? If that were the case, then the question arises as to why Google pays Apple so much money to be installed as the default search engine. How high you rate the quality of search results depends heavily on how much you value genuine search results, in contrast to paid search results. If you compare search results today with search results in the past, you notice that you have to scroll down a long way on your smartphone to reach the genuine search results. Paid search results or results that refer to Google's own services appear top of the list, making sure that you stay within Google's own ecosystem.

Do the big-techs invest large sums of money in innovation? You can safely assume so because their coffers are well filled. The important question, however, is not how much is invested in innovation, but how much innovation there would be in a counterfactual, competitive situation. The theory tells us that if there were competition there would be more innovation because you would use it to attract new customers in order to gain market share. A monopoly does not need this. And there would be other innovations because the innovations would be less geared towards keeping users within the paid area and their own ecosystem, as is currently the case, and not necessarily in the users' interests.

How voluntary is the decision to use these services? It is only voluntary if the user has an attractive alternative. If there is no such alternative because, as described above, it is more difficult for other competitors to enter the market, then the choice is very limited. In the example of Facebook, switching is unattractive if all your friends are on Facebook. In this case, a user does not really have the freedom to switch to another provider while their friends don't switch with them.

Are these services really free? This too is doubtful. Users pay with their data, their attention, and in the end they also pay higher product prices when platforms monopolize the advertising market, thus driving up advertising costs.

In order to strengthen competition in digital markets, in late 2020 the European Commission presented a draft for a Digital Markets Act (DMA), which contains a number of rules that the particularly large platforms must comply with in the future. In summer 2021, five draft laws to increase competition were brought before the US House of Representatives.

Some of the rules provided for in the DMA are aimed at strengthening *competition for markets* in the hope that new providers will use better products to drive out the monopoly. Among other things, this should be made easier by the fact that users can take their data with them when they switch from Facebook to another social media provider, for example. The problem with this rule is that it only has a chance of success if a large number of users switch all at once. The problem is also that, at best, it helps to replace one monopoly with another. Rules that ensure *competition in the market* would, by contrast, be much better. This can be facilitated by the obligation to interoperability.[14] In a specific example, interoperability would mean that if a user switched from Facebook to another provider, they would still have access to their old posts and those of their friends. In this way, they could freely choose their social media provider without having to worry about giving up their network benefits. That would ensure real competition. The draft EU law does not yet provide for such comprehensive interoperability; the US draft goes further.

Proposals not to rely on regulation alone, but to split up the large platforms in cases of doubt go one step further. In the draft EU law, this is currently provided as an option of last resort. One of the five US legislative proposals is much more radical, even if it is currently completely unclear whether the law will ever be passed. The advantage of such a structural regulation compared to the rules of behavior described by the DMA is that it dispenses with the need for time-consuming regulation and constant monitoring. And it doesn't have to mean that it's the end of new, exciting products and innovations, even if the big-tech companies would like you to believe so. This is shown by our investigation of the last breakup in the US, the breakup of AT&T in 1984. At the time, many critics were concerned that after the breakup the telephone service would collapse and the US capacity for innovation would suffer. Exactly the opposite was the case. Phones continued to work and there was a tremendous boom in innovation that paved the way for the Internet age.[15]

However, perhaps the most important aspect in the context of the Convoco topic "How much freedom must we forgo to be free?", which should be considered in the case of big-tech companies in particular, is that if the platforms were broken up, the political power of the tech giants and their owners would be curtailed. And with this we come full circle, because that was a key motivation behind the introduction of antitrust law in the US. It is a concern that should be of particular importance now that a few companies control vast amounts of data. How much freedom does a provider have if they only have access to potential customers via a gatekeeper platform? How much freedom does a citizen have when a single company uses its algorithm to determine the information they receive in response to their search query, which purchase offers are shown to them, which news they can see? My answer is, too little freedom. That is why we need competition as a guarantor of freedom.

Notes

1. Matt Stoller, Biden Launches Sweeping Action on "Big Tech, Big Pharma, and Big Ag." Can It Be Real?, July 11, 2021, https://mattstoller.substack.com/p/biden-launches-sweeping-action-on (accessed November 30, 2021).

2. The White House, "Remarks by President Joe Biden at Signing of an Executive Order Promoting Competition in the American Economy," July 9, 2021, https://www.whitehouse.gov/briefing-room/speeches-remarks/2021/07/09/remarks-by-president-biden-at-signing-of-an-executive-order-promoting-competition-in-the-american-economy/, (accessed November 30, 2021).

3. Tim Wu, *The Curse of Bigness: Antitrust in the New Gilded Age* (New York: Columbia Global Reports, 2018).

4. Amy Klobuchar, *Antitrust: Taking on Monopoly Power from the Gilded Age to the Digital Age* (New York: Random House, 2021).

5. Ibid.

6. Franklin D. Roosevelt, "Message to Congress on Curbing Monopolies," speech of April 29, 1938, https://www.presidency.ucsb.edu/documents/message-congress-curbing-monopolies, (accessed December 7, 2021).

7. Franklin D. Roosevelt, "State of the Union Message to Congress," speech of January 11, 1944, https://www.presidency.ucsb.edu/documents/state-the-union-message-congress, (accessed December 7, 2021).

8. Markus Nagler, Monika Schnitzer, and Martin Watzinger, "Fostering the Diffusion of General Purpose Technologies: Evidence from the Licensing of the Transistor Patents" in *Journal of Industrial Economics*, https://rationality-and-competition.de/wp-content/uploads/2021/11/297.pdf, (accessed November 30, 2021).

9. Thomas Philippon, *The Great Reversal: How America Gave Up on Free Markets* (Cambridge, MA: Harvard University Press, 2019).

10. Philippon, *The Great Reversal*, p. 148.

11. Paul Heidhues et al., "More Competitive Search Through Regulation," Yale Tobin Center for Economic Policy. Digital Regulation Project, Policy Discussion Paper no. 2, 2021, https://tobin.yale.edu/digital-regulation-project, (accessed November 30, 2021).

12. Ibid.

13. Ibid.

14. Amelia Fletcher et al., "Consumer Protection for Online Markets and Large Digital Platforms," Yale Tobin Center for Economic Policy. Digital Regulation Project, Policy Discussion Paper no. 1, 2021, https://tobin.yale.edu/digital-regulation-project, (accessed November 30, 2021).

15. Martin Watzinger and Monika Schnitzer, *The Breakup of the Bell System and its Impact on Innovation* (University of Münster and University of Munich: Mimeo, 2021).

CHAPTER 3

INTERNAL FREEDOM: THE FOX AND THE HEDGEHOG

TIMO MEYNHARDT

Being free and feeling free are not the same thing. What is the point of freedom to supposedly do whatever you like, if you cannot recognize the opportunity or feel overwhelmed by it? Conversely, the ways in which people can maintain their internal freedom, while external restrictions and constraints seem to be impeding it, are well established. Internal and external freedom cannot simply be equated, so anyone who thinks or writes about the shifting concept of freedom, or even makes economic or political decisions "in the name of freedom," must not forget that freedom is essentially an individual experience that can easily elude the externally applied attributes of "free" and "unfree." The statement "I feel free" is highly subjective and full of assumptions to an extent that we ourselves often hardly appreciate. Anyone who dares to venture into the vast sphere of freedom can quickly get into trouble when it comes to generally applied determinations and evaluations of what can be considered "free," what freedom should be measured against, or who makes the decisions.

It is up to us: it is within our grasp to become a little more "free" and independent, at least internally, if we recognize our individual capabilities and limitations and understand ourselves better. In his striking distinction between hedgehogs and foxes, the Russian-Jewish philosopher and historian of ideas Isaiah Berlin made the case for this widely accepted idea of self-knowledge in a remarkable way.[1]

Against the backdrop of Berlin's initial analysis, I would like to show where and how his idea can be applied. As a result, it will become clear how instructive this distinction is to this day, a distinction which Berlin himself claimed was "one of the deepest differences which divide writers and thinkers, and, it may be, human beings in general."[2]

A COMPELLING IDEA

In his brilliant work *The Hedgehog and the Fox: An Essay on Tolstoy's View of History*, Berlin contrasts two ways of thinking. On the one hand it's about trying to recognize connections, dependencies, and causes; on the other it's about attempting to grasp the uniqueness and special qualities of the things that surround us. Berlin vividly traces these two styles of thought through Leo Tolstoy's novel *War and Peace*, using a fragment of verse by the Greek poet Archilochus (680–645 BCE): "The fox knows many things, but the hedgehog knows one big thing."[3] As the history of this essay's impact shows, Berlin succeeded very well in presenting two very different approaches side by side without classifying one as superior to the other.

Berlin's starting point is the following observation:

> For there exists a great chasm between those, on one side, who relate everything to a single central vision, one system, less or more coherent or articulate, in terms of which they understand, think and feel – a single, universal, organizing principle in terms of which alone all that they are and say has significance – and, on the other side, those who pursue many ends, often unrelated and even contradictory, connected, if at all, only in some *de facto* way, for some psychological or physiological cause, related to no moral or

aesthetic principle. These last lead lives, perform acts and entertain ideas that are centrifugal rather than centripetal; their thought is scattered or diffused, moving on many levels, seizing upon the essence of a vast variety of experiences and objects for what they are in themselves, without, consciously or unconsciously, seeking to fit them into, or exclude them from, any one unchanging, all-embracing, sometimes self-contradictory and incomplete, at times fanatical, unitary inner vision.[4]

To put it extremely simply: the hedgehog has answers, while the fox has questions. The former often knows the answer before the question is asked, while the latter has yet another question for every answer. For Berlin, Tolstoy was a fox who "believed in being a hedgehog" (ibid., p. 438). In *War and Peace,* Tolstoy was clearly able to use the conflict resulting from this productively to criticize any attempt to "explain or justify human action or character in terms of social or individual growth or 'roots' in the past" (ibid. p. 443) as superficial or inadequate.

In the epilogue to the second part of the novel, Tolstoy offers an incisive explanation of how history develops:

The new history is like a deaf man replying to questions which nobody puts to him . . . the primary question . . . is, what power is it that moves the destinies of peoples? . . . History seems to presuppose that this power can be taken for granted, and is familiar to everyone, but, in spite of every wish to admit that this power is familiar to us, anyone who has read a great many historical works cannot help doubting whether this power, which different historians understand in different ways, is in fact so completely familiar to everyone.[5]

According to Berlin, Tolstoy exhibits this skeptical, nihilistic attitude towards decisive action, the formative role of the individual or towards assigning blame as a sharp-eyed fox who wants to expose legal statements as hollow, regards practicability as an illusion, and refuses all abstraction or synthesis. Instead, he is concerned with "'live' experience," whose uniqueness he describes with an almost unsurpassable precision.

Tolstoy does an excellent job of pointing out the weaknesses of the hedgehog, who misses a lot because he finds it difficult to think outside the conceptual box, to be surprised, to think in terms of alternatives, and not to insist on a valid explanation. At the same time—and this is the productive power of the conflict—Tolstoy was well aware of the fox's equally limited vision and spent his life searching—desperately in the end—for a monistic view of life "bitterly intent upon seeing in the manner of a hedgehog" (ibid., p. 493). But here Tolstoy ultimately failed, or in Berlin's words: "Tolstoy's sense of reality was until the end too devastating to be compatible with any moral ideal" (ibid., p. 498). In the end, the great artist and highly revered writer is "a desperate old man, beyond human aid, wandering self-blinded at Colonus" (ibid., p. 498).

Berlin sees in Tolstoy

> a bitter inner conflict between his actual experience and his beliefs, between his vision of life and his theory of what it, and he himself, ought to be if the vision was to be bearable at all; between the immediate data, which he was too honest and too intelligent to ignore, and the need for an interpretation of them which did not lead to the childish absurdities of all previous views.[6]

These extremes demonstrate how mutually conflicting different motives and ways of thinking can be. In general, Berlin succeeds remarkably in using the hedgehog–fox distinction to grasp the contradictions inherent in the person of Leo Tolstoy and thus make comprehensible the way of thinking that shapes the understanding of history in *War and Peace*. This is all the more exceptional because other completely different theoretical frames of reference would have been available. We might think, for example, of an explanation using the history of political science or an interpretation using psychopathology, in particular of an affective disorder like manic depression.

The great strength of the hedgehog–fox distinction is that it neither evaluates content (as in the history of political science) nor judges normatively (as in a psychopathological view).

Overall, in his widely acclaimed work on Tolstoy's tragic foxiness, I think that Isaiah Berlin made a contribution to understanding human (un)freedom that was at least as important as his distinction between positive and negative freedom.[7] His essay on Tolstoy shows one thing above all: it is up to us to recognize the characteristics of our view of ourselves and the world and to move the boundaries.

CURRENT RELEVANCE

Since it was first published, Isaiah Berlin's basic idea has developed a life of its own and has long since become disconnected from its original context. For example, in his study on predicting political events, the psychologist Philip Tetlock has showed that those experts whose style of thinking corresponded to that of the fox made more realistic judgments.[8] Apparently it pays to be open to different points of view, to resist hasty generalizations, and to be able to accept several versions of the truth. However, according to Tetlock's findings the hedgehog is given more public recognition for his clarity and visionary power. It is therefore not surprising that fewer foxes than hedgehogs occupy the top positions in business and politics, as another study suggests.[9] If you want to get to the top, you obviously need a clear profile. Ambiguity and doubt are quickly interpreted as weakness. Inevitably, alternative ways of thinking have to take a back seat and contradictions minimized. In a complex world, you must be careful when reducing actions or events to a few basic principles. Typical hedgehog attitudes are reflected in statements such as: "At the end of the day, it's always just about ABC" or "Ultimately, only XYZ counts."

While Tetlock assumed in his study that there is a continuum and that more hedgehog-thinking leads to less fox-thinking, it has now been shown that some people are perfectly able to move back and forth between the two ways of thinking, or are able to think along the lines of the other side.[10] This surmounting of the dichotomy is also much closer to Berlin's characterization of Tolstoy's thinking. However, he found it impossible not just to perceive the hedgehog side as a blank space, but to cast it in a positive light. The manifestation of such a hybrid way of thinking obviously requires the meta-ability of being mindful of one's own style of thinking and the mental flexibility to consciously adopt the other perspective. This is an ideal that has to be carried out in practice and can often be triggered only by a specific change in social context or a crisis of the individual. In this sense, it is less about what a person thinks and more about how they deal with information and organize experiences.

There now exists a tried and tested procedure for analyzing one's own way of thinking.[11] Based on the individual's own assessment of the extent to which the following statements apply, each person's tendency can be reliably identified:

1. I usually make important decisions quickly and confidently.
2. Even after I have made up my mind about something, I am always eager to consider a different opinion.
3. I prefer interacting with people whose opinions are very different to my own.
4. It is annoying to listen to someone who cannot seem to make up his or her mind.
5. When considering most conflict situations, I can usually see how both sides could be right.
6. Having clear rules and order at work is essential for success.

Instructions on how to carry out and evaluate this analysis can be found in the Notes.[12]

A few examples show how stimulating this analysis of thinking style is for the questions being asked today in a wide variety of disciplines. While Stephen Jay Gould[13] uses the image of the fox and the hedgehog to illuminate the relationship between the humanities and the natural sciences, Jim Collins[14] sees the "hedgehog concept" as one secret to the success of good management. In a similarly positive approach to hedgehog thinking, Ronald Dworkin[15] calls for "justice for hedgehogs" and argues for mutually supportive values that together create a truth about living well. By contrast, John Kay[16] points out the fox's advantage in taking detours to reach its destination, and Nate Silver[17] shows how hedgehogs are often their own worst enemies when it comes to their predictions. Daniel Kahneman[18] too takes a critical approach to the "hedgehog effect."

Mitchell and Tetlock argue[19] that judges with a preference for fox-thinking view problems from different perspectives and consider a variety of information and interests. Judges with hedgehog tendencies are less likely to think in this way, focusing on just a few key pieces of evidence, and aiming less frequently for compromise.

We could easily add to this list. In conclusion, two findings from basic psychological research are worth noting. It has been found that hedgehogness in thinking tends to increase with age, which seems entirely plausible. It was also found that those people who think in a hybrid way (high levels of both orientations at the same time) perceive the contribution of their organization to the common good more powerfully. This was recorded across a variety of dimensions. This finding is interesting because it shows how perceiving diversity and unity simultaneously can combine to form an overall impression (in this case the common good).[20]

In sum, we cannot ignore how, especially in the Anglo-American world, Archilochos' line of verse as used by Isaiah Berlin is applied again and again to describe and explain very different phenomena in mental activity. It obviously gets to the heart of something that is intuitively understandable and at the same time offers added value in terms of analysis. Berlin—himself a fox—wasn't sure at first how far the distinction would go. The reason for its continued success may lie in the combination of the idea's openness to interpretation and the symbolic power of the animal image.

ON THE ROAD TO INTERNAL FREEDOM

Isaiah Berlin began his essay by citing the following phrase: "A queer combination of the brain of an English chemist with the soul of an Indian Buddhist," and his entire text can be read as an attempt to do justice to both. This requires internal freedom and equanimity to tolerate and accept the other person's view of things.

Examining one's own patterns of thought and reaction is not always pleasant; the results may be rejected or even suppressed. However, the best outcome enables a gain in freedom that should not be underestimated: by discovering something as "typical" for me, I can distance myself from it and look at it from a different perspective. The crucial thing is to question your own point of view and no longer see it as immutable. At the same time, this can increase the chances of finding new solutions, but it can also be deeply unsettling if what was previously taken for granted is lost.

As Berlin argues, throughout his life Tolstoy did not find a viable way of balancing his pronounced foxiness and reducing dissonance in such a way that diversity and unity could exist side by side on an equal footing. However, without a heightened awareness of the conflict, he probably would not have attained his enormous success as a writer, of which *War and Peace* is a unique testimony. In this respect, gaining internal freedom by better understanding one's own way of thinking remains a double-edged sword.

Bearing in mind the opportunities, however, it is true that the ability to mediate between the two styles, to recognize both as valuable, and to transcend the conflict between one's own preferences cannot be overestimated. In particular, achieving a hybrid style of thinking has its advantages. Philip Tetlock even suggests that super-forecasters (people who can predict events as they develop much better than the general public or experts) "combine the best of foxiness and hedgehoginess."[21]

Dealing with our own mental flexibility should allow us to break down prejudices against other points of view, to treat them with respect, and to be able to let differences remain. This is perhaps the most important outcome of a self-generated, internal freedom: you are free if you liberate yourself from either-or thinking, hasty evaluations, and knee-jerk reactions. In a world full of contradictions and conflicts, the internal freedom gained through self-reflection is more important than abstract declarations of freedom. This can be seen in a confident way of dealing with other points of view and in not limiting oneself through emotional overreactions (anger, aggression, or fear). This does not mean enduring everything with stoic equanimity or regarding every truth as relative, but it does mean accepting the irreconcilability of values—Berlin called this "objective pluralism"— and constantly searching for what we mean by humanity and a shared humanity. Committing oneself to such a common good does not mean abandoning the self. Rather, it is in one's own interest, since no one can live without a conducive and supportive environment.

This topic is particularly explosive today in light of current crises, in which it is unclear where the limits to expressing a variety of opinions lie and where a uniform perspective places disproportionate restrictions on the freedom of the individual. These limits have to be renegotiated time and again when embarking upon new territory. Even if the transitions are fluid, pragmatic demarcations remain necessary in order to defuse any conflicts that might arise. To do this we need individuals who are internally free and independent, who appreciate both sides (hybrid way of thinking), and who use common sense to contribute to a common good that strengthens the individual. Conversely, however, there should also be room for different styles of thinking—for hedgehogs and foxes alike—in our notions of the common good.

Let's sum up the thesis of this article. Our personal idiosyncrasies—using the example of our way of thinking—make us "unfree" if they prevent us from taking on board other perspectives. The example of Isaiah Berlin's distinction between the fox and the hedgehog has made it clear how appealing but also challenging it can be to throw old certainties overboard. The hedgehog's great strength is that he can get straight to the point, while the fox benefits from being able to accept multiple perspectives at the same time. However, we should neither curl up with our comfortable truths nor get bogged down foxily between several claims to truth. We become freer internally when we have the courage to challenge ourselves again and again and organize our experiences in new ways. In the best-case scenario, we will become more confident and can make a more effective contribution in situations where freedom is under threat. We could also say that the way to more external freedom is via greater internal freedom.

Notes

1. Isaiah Berlin, *The Hedgehog and the Fox: An Essay on Tolstoy's View of History* https://www.blogs.hss.ed.ac.uk/crag/files/2016/06/the_hedgehog_and_the_fox-berlin.pdf (accessed January 19, 2022).

2. Berlin, *The Hedgehog and the Fox*, p. 436.

3. According to his biographer, Berlin was alerted to this quotation by a university friend, Lord Oxford. As a student of ancient philosophy, Lord Oxford considered this verse to have "all the elegance and mystery of a Japanese haiku." Michael Ignatieff, *Isaiah Berlin: A Life* (London: Vintage, 2000), p. 173.

4. Berlin, *The Hedgehog and the Fox*, pp. 436–37.

5. Quoted in Berlin, *The Hedgehog and the Fox*, p. 453.

6. Berlin, *The Hedgehog and the Fox*, p. 463.

7. The earlier and better known distinction between negative freedom (freedom from) and positive freedom (freedom to) was discussed by Berlin initially in his inaugural lecture in Oxford in 1958, this influencing subsequent debates to a considerable extent. See Isaiah Berlin, *Liberty* (Oxford: Oxford University Press, 2002).

8. Philip E. Tetlock, *Expert Political Judgment: How Good Is It? How Can We Know?*, Princeton: Princeton University Press, 2005).

9. Peter Gomez and Timo Meynhardt, "More Foxes in the Boardroom: Systems Thinking in Action" in *Systemic Management for Intelligent Organizations*, ed. Stefan N. Grösser and René Zeier (Berlin and Heidelberg: Springer, 2012), pp. 83–98.

10. Timo Meynhardt, Carolin Hermann, and Stefan Anderer, "Making Sense of a Most Popular Metaphor in Management: Towards a HedgeFox Scale for Cognitive Styles" in *Administrative Sciences* 7, 2017, pp. 1–23.

11. Ibid.

12. Here's how to determine your style of thinking in four steps:

    1) Self-assessment: answer all the questions. If the statement applies, write down a 6, if it does not apply at

all, write down a 1. Use the numbers in between to grade your assessment.

2) Then add up the numerical values of statement 1, statement 4, and statement 6 to calculate the extent of your "hedgehogness." Then add up the numerical values of statement 2, statement 3, and statement 5 in order to calculate the extent of your "foxiness."

3) Identifying your thinking style: four variants can occur. Please use the numerical values to determine the one that applies to you:

Hedgehog: the foxiness dimension is between 3 and 12; the hedgehogness dimension is between 15 and 18.

Fox: the foxiness dimension is between 13 and 18; the hedgehogness dimension is between 3 and 14.

HedgeFox: the foxiness dimension is between 13 and 18; the hedgehogness dimension between 15 and 18.

No dominant profile: the foxiness dimension is between 3 and 12; the hedgehogness dimension between 3 and 14.

4) Interpretation: Please decide for yourself, or preferably with someone you trust, how characteristic your profile is for you. It is advisable to visualize your own style through concrete examples. The procedure does not replace comprehensive psychological diagnostics, but it is a reliable way of revealing initial tendencies that can provide important clues for self-reflection.

13. Stephen Jay Gould, *The Hedgehog, the Fox, and the Magister's Pox: Mending and Minding the Misconceived Gap between Science and the Humanities* (New York: Vintage, 2003).

14. Jim C. Collins, *Good to Great. Why Some Companies Make the Leap... and Others Don't* (New York: Random House, 2001).

15. Ronald Dworkin, *Justice for Hedgehogs* (Cambridge MA: The Belknap Press of Harvard University Press, 2011).

16. John Kay, *Obliquity. Why Our Goals are Best Achieved Indirectly* (London: Profile, 2011).

17. Nate Silver, *The Signal and the Noise. Why So Many Predictions Fail—But Some Don't* (New York: Penguin, 2015).

18. Daniel Kahneman, *Thinking, Fast and Slow* (New York: Penguin, 2013).

19. Gregory Mitchell and Philip E. Tetlock, "Cognitive Style and Judging" in *The Psychology of Judicial Decision-Making*, ed. David E. Klein and Gregory Mitchell (Oxford: Oxford University Press, 2010), pp. 279–84.

20. Meynhardt et al., "Making Sense of a Most Popular Metaphor in Management: Towards a HedgeFox Scale for Cognitive Styles."

21. Philip E. Tetlock, in a personal message of February 26, 2016: "I suspect you are on to something very important I missed. My sense is that the best forecasters in the super-forecasting project combine the best of foxiness and hedgehoginess, which connects nicely to the concept in management of cognitive ambidexterity. No hard data to support any of this—just a hunch."

CHAPTER 4

FREEDOM OF SPEECH AND FREEDOM OF THOUGHT

TIM CRANE

Is there a crisis of freedom of speech today? My answer is that if there is a crisis, it's not about freedom of speech as such. It is rather that many concerns about freedom of speech can indicate something that is much more serious. Freedom of speech matters, because freedom of thought matters.

It's common today to hear it said that freedom of speech is in crisis. I am talking here mostly about the United States and Britain, but I also believe that a lot of these discussions are going on in Germany and Austria too. Moreover, we hear talk of crisis from people on the left and on the right of the political spectrum. On the right, we find a reaction to what's become known as the "woke ideology" (the latest manifestation of what used to be called political correctness) or "cancel culture" and to things that, broadly speaking, fall under the heading of identity politics. On the left we also see, particularly in the United States, a left-wing response to right-wing objections to so-called "critical race theory" and other phenomena. The response is that these objections interfere with academic freedom, or with educational freedom and freedom of speech. Both sides, in what is known today as the culture wars, appeal to the value of freedom of speech. But what is the value of freedom of speech? Why does it matter? Why is free speech valuable at all? Why should it matter whether we can say what we like? In the American context, there's a quick answer to this: freedom of speech is a right, it's a human right, protected by the Constitution. The US Constitution's First Amendment, written in 1791, specifies that "Congress shall make no law abridging the freedom of speech."

Of course, this doesn't help those of us who don't live in a country with this as a constitutional right. This doesn't answer the question of the importance of freedom of speech. But an interesting thing is that, in America, it is common for appeals to freedom of speech to be made as a response to certain problems, which on the face of it don't have much to do with freedom of speech. American debates can turn very quickly into debates about First Amendment rights even when they started out being about other things. There was an extraordinary example of this in the 1980s, when the distinguished legal philosopher Ronald Dworkin defended the right of pornographers to produce pornography on the grounds that this was protected by First Amendment rights. This is really rather strange: why is this a debate about freedom of speech, as opposed to being a debate about the freedom to produce pornographic material, or about whether there should be such a freedom? What has it got to do with speech? I mention this to draw attention to the widespread use of appeals to freedom of speech in discussions in the United States, even when speech is not really an issue.

These discussions rarely explain why freedom of speech matters and why it is such an absolute, inviolable right. In fact, there must be limits to freedom of speech. No one should believe that any kind of speech at all should be permitted at any time, in any place, by any person. I should not have the right to stand in a public space and broadcast obscenities 24 hours a day very loudly. No one should have that right. So freedom of speech cannot be an inviolable right, nor should it be. This is because when we have a conflict of values, a conflict of rights, other values can override the value of freedom of speech.

Yet this doesn't answer the question of why free speech is a value at all. Why should it matter? Why should it be so important? I think the strongest answer to this question is the liberal answer: freedom of speech is a value because freedom itself is a fundamental value. It's a value whose importance and significance to us cannot be explained in other terms. That, in short, is what it means when we say freedom is fundamental. Liberals say that the state should interfere with individual freedom as little as possible. If John Stuart Mill is right in his famous essay *On Liberty* (1859), interference with people's freedom should only be permitted in order to prevent harm to others. This is the famous "harm principle" central to Mill's liberalism. So the answer then is that the value of freedom of speech derives from the value of freedom as such. I'm not saying that the explanation of the value of freedom will be a simple thing, but only that freedom of speech matters because freedom matters, and that this will also be the beginning of the explanation of why freedom of speech should sometimes be limited. Freedom of speech may be limited, liberals will say, because such speech may cause harm to others, or because other values may be more important in the context. Freedom of speech as such is not an ultimate value.

What are debates about freedom of speech really about? My claim is that frequently they're not really about freedom of speech. Sometimes, debates apparently about freedom of speech are really about whether harm is likely to be caused by the expression of some ideas in speech. This would explain why some people are concerned to limit speech—because they think harm is being caused—and others are not so concerned—because they think that no harm is being caused. The question is about the existence of harm in a specific context, not about freedom of speech. The parties in a debate like this may well agree about freedom of speech, even if they say they do not. So this should be the question for liberals, not the question about whether we have an absolute or immutable right to freedom of speech. This is just as well, since debates about the absolute value of freedom of speech go round in circles very quickly, as anyone who's been involved in these discussions knows. What we need to look at is the question of harm, and how much harm is actually caused by people speaking in certain ways. Of course, this is not a simple question either—but it's a very specific question and it can be addressed empirically.

A good start would be to accept that it cannot be that harm is caused to someone by speech just because they think or feel that they have been harmed.

However, I now want to move on to what may be a deeper point about freedom, which goes beyond this familiar point about the restriction of speech based on harm. My point is that one danger of restricting freedom of speech is that it can also restrict freedom of thought. Broadly speaking, this is because what people are capable of thinking is conditioned by the range of concepts they have and the words they use. I'm not saying that people are incapable of thinking without words. Lots of thinking doesn't occur in words, and many animals who lack a language can still think in some way. But the distinctively human ability to use words is what gives our thought its depth and richness.

When language is compelled or forbidden, this can erode the capacity to think. I'll give a contemporary example. The word "cisgender" is used in debates about gender and sexuality these days to mean something like "those people who identify with the gender conventionally associated with their biological sex." If you identify with the conventional associations of being a woman or being a man, then you are a cisgender person.

People who like to talk in this way say that anyone who isn't transgender—that is anyone who doesn't identify with the conventional associations linked to their biological sex—is actually cisgender. Many people object to that by saying that they don't identify with any conventional marks of gender and sexuality at all; they may even want to resist the whole idea of identifying as belonging to a certain gender. They might want to say that the whole idea of identifying with a gender role is dubious and should be treated with suspicion. But, if we are obliged to talk in terms of cisgender, then this skepticism cannot be expressed. If you are given a forced choice between describing yourself as cisgender or transgender, then the only way to deny that you are associating with the conventional gender roles attached to your biological sex is to say that you are not cisgender. And that, according to this way of thinking, makes you transgender—which is not what you intended.

Suppose you don't want to identify with any gender at all. Suppose you want to say that you don't identify with the traditional gender roles associated with your biological sex. You might want to reject the idea that anyone has to adopt traditional gender roles associated with belonging to either sex. According to the exclusive and exhaustive distinction between cisgender and transgender, there is no way to express this without committing yourself to being transgender. But since that idea is usually defined in terms of the idea of gender identity too, this is not what you wanted to say. This might affect your ability to think through your own situation and attitudes properly. Imposing what seemed like a clear and well-intended distinction can make it difficult for you to think the things you want to think.

We can make the point using an analogy with the concept of cultural appropriation. Cultural appropriation is the idea of taking an element from one culture and incorporating it into one's own culture. It may be an artistic element, a concept, a visual image, or clothing, and so on. It is sometimes claimed that cultural appropriation is always a mistake or something that needs to be eliminated through education. More precisely, the fault is usually taking something from the culture of oppressed people or from a culture or civilization less powerful than one's own. It's plain that such cultural appropriation can be done in ways that are degrading or insulting to people, as in the offensive practice of white people putting on "blackface." But it seems to me that what's wrong with this is because it's degrading or insulting, not because it's cultural appropriation. The mere idea that you can take things from other cultures and incorporate them into your own culture cannot itself be something that is bad in itself. In fact, it is actually the source of much of the creativity in human cultures. To exaggerate perhaps a little, without cultural appropriation, art or cuisine—food as we know it—would be impossible. My analogy here is that those who think that cultural appropriation is a bad thing are trying to force people to think in a certain way, and in doing so they've closed off opportunities for creative thinking. They've closed off the legitimate opportunity for people to take ideas or images from wherever they like and create something possibly beautiful, wonderful, or interesting. They've also closed off opportunities for bad thinking too, that is true. But both of those things come together when you have freedom of thought. How to deal with the cruel or offensive versions of cultural appropriation is another matter. The point of the analogy is only to illustrate how freedom of thought might depend on freedom of speech.

George Orwell's term "thoughtcrime" is a good word for this phenomenon. It's one thing to restrict what people can say in public. It's a very different thing to regulate what they should think. In a striking recent case of life imitating art, a man in the UK was interviewed by the police because of things he had written on social media. Although the police acknowledged that he had committed no crime, they said "we need to check your thinking." Let that sink in: the police in Britain—a democracy with a long established tradition of individual liberty—are checking up on what people are thinking. Orwell memorably described how totalitarian states attempt to regulate how people think. To see this starting to happen—in a small way, but it is happening—in Orwell's own country is really quite alarming. My suggestion is that forcing people to talk in certain ways can force them to think in certain ways. This takes time; it doesn't happen immediately. But it can happen, and it is deeply illiberal. If we want to hold onto liberal principles at all, we must resist this idea that you can compel people to think in certain ways, even if their thoughts are objectionable.

The heart of liberalism, it seems to me, is the concept of tolerance. Tolerance is something that is often misunderstood. Sometimes tolerance is described as the notion that all views are equally valid, or that everyone's views deserve respect. Of course, if that's what tolerance means, then tolerance is a bad thing: not all views deserve respect; not all views are equally valid. But this is not what tolerance really is. In fact, tolerance is coming to terms with the existence of something that you object to. It is of the essence of tolerance that you object to what you are tolerating. I tolerate my neighbor's occasional loud music because I want to live in peace with them. I don't "tolerate" the abolition of torture, which is something I strongly believe in. Toleration is putting up with something to some further end. I will end my reflections with some thoughts about toleration and freedom and their relation to one another.

An interesting fact about toleration is that the origin of religious toleration and the origin of liberalism arose together, at the same time. It's a commonplace to say that religious tolerance emerged in Western Europe after the Wars of Religion in the 16th and 17th centuries, because the state realized it could not force belief upon people. This is expressed in the definition of the French word *tolérance* in the Académie Française first dictionary in 1694. *Tolérance* is defined as "sufferance, forbearance that one has for what one cannot prevent." So the original idea was that one tolerates what one cannot prevent.

But within 100 years, the failure to prevent these things—the failure to compel people to believe the same things—was turned into a success. The success was the creation of religious liberty, the right to religious freedom. This is what you find in Article 10 of the *Declaration of the Rights of Man* (1789): "No one should be disturbed for his opinions, even in religion, provided that their manifestation does not trouble public order as established by law." So tolerance as forbearance, putting up with something that you can't change, was turned into a right of human beings. And note the crucial distinction expressed here: between opinions and their "manifestations," that is, between ideas themselves and their expression in speech and writing. If we then go back to the First Amendment of the US Constitution (1791), we can see that the first thing that's mentioned is religious freedom. So, around the same time as the French declaration, freedom of religion was regarded in the American Bill of Rights as a fundamental right: "Congress shall make no law respecting an establishment of religion." Notice that the first thing—the First Amendment—is about freedom of religion, that is freedom of *belief*, freedom of thought. It seems to me that this important point is often overlooked in discussions of this First Amendment and freedom of speech, in the US and elsewhere.

We can learn something from the history of religious tolerance and its relation to freedom of speech. A liberal state can of course legitimately prohibit certain forms of speech if they genuinely cause harm. But the state cannot and should not compel belief. This will have unhappy consequences, because people will believe bad and vile things. But if you agree with me that the state should not "check your thinking," then you should agree that compulsion or restriction of thought should not be part of a liberal state. We tolerate those opinions that we object to; but these opinions might not deserve respect. That's a very important fact about toleration, and about our attitude to others. In a sense, we may respect the people who hold the opinions, but we don't have to respect their opinions. We might be disappointed that we can't control the beliefs of others, but we have to accept that this is a fundamental consequence of genuine freedom.

CHAPTER 5

ARE HUMAN FREEDOM AND AUTONOMY JUST AN ILLUSION?

HERBERT A. REITSAMER

INTRODUCTION

A basic requirement for enjoying freedom is the ability to make decisions and carry out actions freely, that is having free will. For such free will to be possible, we need a consciousness that allows us to identify with our physical shell and the information stored in our brain and to perceive ourselves as a person. Legally, this all seems resolved, as the legislature does indeed attribute the ability to understand, make judgments, and act only to people who have free will. If this is not the case, the individual does not have legal capacity. This definition confirms the value of our subjective human self-image, as we see ourselves as self-determined individuals.

Just a few years ago the debate about the existence or lack of free will was a hot topic for philosophers and neuroscientists. From antiquity to modern times, great thinkers have addressed the question of free will and, through their discussions, they have shed light on the issues in a wide variety of ways. Early on, Greek philosophers addressed this topic through a reasoned dilemma. Two schools of thought consider free will to be incompatible with determinism. The libertarians believe in free will and therefore reject determinism; taking a fundamentally deterministic stance, the determinists do not believe in free will—both are incompatibilists. Compatibilists think that determinism does not pose an insurmountable contradiction to free will and consider these two attitudes to be reconcilable. We should, however, be cautious when comparing the findings of the Greek philosophers with today's debates, because the anthropological concept of free will was only formulated by Augustine (344–430 CE).[1] In the Greek philosophers' terminology there was no concept that was directly comparable with free will;

they referred instead to drive, preparation, planning, and other similar concepts.

In his theory of atomism, Democritus (460–370 BCE) provided the material basis for determinism. As well as divine influence on cosmic events, he also indirectly rejected free will, because in a deterministic world in which all states can be traced back precisely to the movements of elementary atoms, the argument in favor of free will is not conclusively possible and even irreconcilable with such a world. A solution had to be found, and so the Greek philosopher Epicurus (341–271 BCE) introduced the notion of uncertainty into the cosmic order with a remarkable argument and without the help of empirically measured data in order to make freedom possible. More than two thousand years later, one of the pioneers of quantum mechanics, Werner Heisenberg, expressed this uncertainty of the simultaneous determinability of the position and momentum of a particle in the "Heisenberg uncertainty principle." We now know that the neurons in our brain do not have a 100 percent activation threshold and also that synaptic activity is subject to neural noise. So the exact temporal point of synaptic transmission can only be determined with a degree of uncertainty. Chance therefore plays a role in the processing of neural signals.

NEUROSCIENTIFIC ISSUES

The triumph of free will was thus advancing unimpeded, until a new empirical science, neurophysiology, took to the stage, seriously disrupting the relative calm that had returned to academic discourse in the interim. The idea of a brain with precisely localizable areas and allocated functions corresponds to our desire to describe the most complicated relationships using the simplest possible formulae and explanations—an $E = mc^2$ for neurobiology would be extremely welcome. It turned out, however, that a much greater number of areas of the brain than just the primary areas of our neocortex perform the tasks of creating associations. They include the basal ganglia with their gatekeeper role, which form part of the visual and auditory pathways or of motor and cognitive processing; or the limbic system (a complex interconnection of various different parts of the brain), where, among other things, the processing and formation of emotions and drives as well as memory content takes place, and much more. It is important to realize that these areas handle a wide variety of neural processes that are linked together in close networks. The brain's processing work is therefore highly complex and it is difficult to draw wide-ranging conclusions from simple experiments. For example, a large part of the entire brain is involved in the processing of visual sensory impressions, as well as in the planning, control, and execution of complex movements.

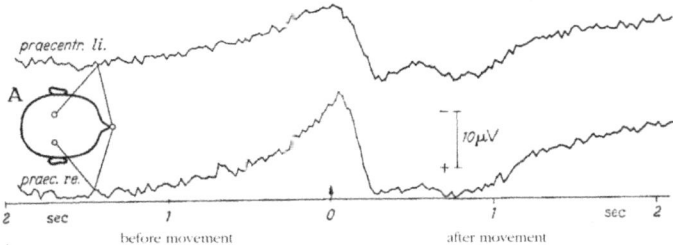

Fig. 1 *Changes in the brain potential in voluntary movements of the left hand. The movement begins at temporal point 0 (arrow). Readiness potential builds up before the movement begins, which reaches larger amplitude above the right hemisphere than above the left. Average of 512 movements. Negativity upwards. Left of 0 = time before the onset of the movement in the electromyogram. Drawing modified after Kornhuber and Deecke.*[2]

In 1964, neuroscientists Lüder Deecke and Hans Helmut Kornhuber discovered the "readiness potential," a form of electrical activity revealed by the electroencephalogram (EEG), which shows the activity of nerve cells above a certain region of the brain called the supplementary motor area (SMA), and which precedes the onset of a movement (fig. 1). This potential can increase slowly up to 1.5 seconds before a hand movement is carried out.[3] The neural processes on which this potential is based relate to drive and motivation, attention and planning of the movement to be carried out, and much more. This scientific work laid the foundation for further research on motor drive, attention, planning, and execution, as its findings raised a number of new questions. Subjectively we may experience the time between our conscious decision and the subsequent execution of a movement as significantly shorter than the time periods suggested by Kornhuber and Deecke.

As a result, Benjamin Libet, a neurophysiologist at the University of San Francisco, decided to carry out some more experiments. He set his test subjects the following task: they were to make a hand movement at a moment chosen by them at random within a certain time interval. The temporal occurrence of the following variables was also analyzed:

1. As in Kornhuber and Deecke's experiment, the readiness potential above the SMA was measured in the test subjects' EEG (see fig. 1).
2. The test subjects had to look at a clock face and note the position of the hand (a circling point of light) at the moment they became aware that they now wanted to perform the movement.

3. Muscle activity was measured by determining the electrical activity of the hand muscles.

The moment was not known to the scientist. However, the EEG potentials identified during these investigations clearly showed that the moment of this voluntary finger movement could be predicted by a readiness potential—not in all cases, but statistically significantly better than at random. The analysis of all variables showed that the brain was already showing neural activities in the form of readiness potentials that occurred before the conscious decision to act. So the decision to move was taken—at least in part—unconsciously.[4]

Libet's studies had a disruptive impact on all libertarians who saw the results of these investigations as a threat to the existence of free will. Not everyone appreciated their new sparring partner, and terms such as "neuromafia" were bandied about. Nevertheless, Libet's results were confirmed by further experiments conducted using functional magnetic resonance imaging (fMRI) and by measurements made using deep brain electrodes. It was even shown that neural activities could already be measured by fMRI several seconds before the decision to perform a movement. However, it could also be shown that up to a certain "point of no return" it is possible to revoke and interrupt the decision to carry out a movement. There have always been differences of opinion about the nature of human freedom and free will, and on this occasion, evidence provided by the natural sciences added a powerful argument, thus changing the basis of further debates.

Critics asked whether the findings of the experiments by Libet and his successors would justify questioning the existence of free will. Critics argued that finger movements in scenarios with few alternatives, in which only the moment for deciding to move was available, have little to do with the real world. Motivation and planning were low and the actions could be expected to have neither positive nor negative consequences. Furthermore, it was not necessary to make complex trade-offs and consider several alternatives. In the case of simple movements that we often carry out, there is no need for any time-consuming build-up to the movement through planning etc., as such movements are almost automatic and can be carried out with our cerebellum (motor memory) playing a significant role. In such movements there is much less active adaptation of motor skills via feedback and readjustment in the cortex. In the case of precisely planned movements, in which we pay attention to the exact execution and we have to process feedback from the visual system, pressure receptors, heat and pain receptors, vibration sensors, and input from depth sensitivity, our consciousness is subject to great demands and takes on a much more active role than in the case of actions that are carried out almost as reflexes.

COMPLEXITY AND INTERPOLATION

Psychological studies have clearly shown that we can be influenced in our decision-making. Due to the enormous amount of information that flows into "us" from our sensory systems, our memory, or our genetic predisposition, it is extremely important that our conscious processes are supported by the unconscious processing of information. Imagine having to completely rationalize every gut feeling or intuition in order to be able to act. Apart from the fact that this is almost impossible, making quick decisions under such circumstances would only be possible to a very limited extent. Human beings have sensory systems that have feedback loops built into their processing pathways. This means that our memories and previous neural experiences influence the processing of our sense impressions via learning processes (for example, advertising, but also any other kind of experience and learnt behavior). So our sense impressions are modulated by the content of our memories. There is a kind of bias towards the way sense impressions or memories and unconscious memories are perceived. Put simply, we could say that we construct a subjective truth by our brain suggesting the most plausible solutions.

A concrete example shows how what we perceive is supplemented by memory content and how these supplements can be misleading. We know the situation in which we see a person indistinctly in a crowd, get a brief impression of a face, and then suddenly think we recognize the person. Although it lacks the quantity of information needed to make a reliable identification, our brain has proposed a solution. Unconsciously processed key stimuli helped form the face or the impression of the person into a recognizable structure. The missing parts were supplemented from our memory and put together to form the person we know—but on second glance, it wasn't this person. So it is also possible that different eyewitnesses report different things about the same course of events.[5] The witnesses told the subjective truth to the best of their knowledge and belief, and yet these subjective truths can differ from one another and from the actual course of events.

Motorists are familiar with another phenomenon. You drive down a street, lost in thought, and suddenly wonder how you have negotiated the last few bends ("highway hypnosis").[6] Although we performed it unconsciously, we would probably not assume that this act of driving was not done through our free will. Despite the complexity of the process, perception, motivation, planning, and the resulting activation of our muscles happened unconsciously. In this situation, the unconscious steering of the vehicle replaced conscious action. How the unconscious communicates with the conscious and how neural patterns reach the level of consciousness is still the subject of intense research.

CONSCIOUSNESS

The prerequisite for a conscious perception might, for example, be reaching a certain threshold of neural activity. If groups of neurons are supplied with information by a sensory system, the neurons in these groups must remain active in order to be consciously perceived and be consolidated for the memory. These are groups of neurons that can comprise thousands of individual cells. Each of the 100 billion or so neurons in our brain creates up to 10,000 synapses with other neurons. The number of synaptic connections is estimated to be over 100 trillion and the number of possible connections resulting from this is beyond astronomical. Only the neural connections that are frequently activated and therefore particularly important remain in our brain as engrams—thought traces that connect groups of neurons physiologically. Every sense impression results in an engram, thus altering our brain. In order to enable (self-)awareness, a continuous flow of memory and thus also the possibility of creating a temporally and spatially continuous identification with the past, the projected future, and the physical shell of a person must take place.

So, must free will necessarily be based solely on conscious decisions? Is it not sufficient for unconscious processes to go hand in hand with conscious processes, with the unconscious process supporting the conscious one? We don't know the answer to that. However, scientists are increasingly of the opinion that the sometimes unconscious initiation of movements does not challenge the freedom to decide whether to carry out a movement. The exact role consciousness plays in these decisions, however, is still unclear.

Psychiatrist and author Iain McGilchrist believes that the subconscious is just as much a part of a person as their consciousness. He sees no reason why free will should not be socialized with deeper, unconscious processes, and therefore does not find any contradiction to free will when carrying out a movement.[7]

ISSUES IN QUANTUM PHYSICS

In order to better understand the source of freedom as a scientist, the quantum physicist Hans Briegel and his then doctoral student Gemma De las Cuevas of the University of Innsbruck put forward a new model of the memory and related aspects of free will. The scientists see no contradiction between the biological processes taking place in the brain within the framework of the laws of nature and the freedom to make decisions. To facilitate this, they introduced chance into their model, as Epicurus had done before them. They showed that naturally or artificially operating systems with a certain degree of physical or biological organization can very well develop a free will.[8] The basis for their model is the content of memory, which is not continuous but organized in snapshots ("clips"), as described in Francis Crick and Christof Koch's hypothesis.[9] This episodic, compositional memory system was represented using a stochastic dynamic model. Memory contents related to certain situations are recalled randomly. These retrievals happen with a certain degree of probability, which can change as the system learns. One essential characteristic is that the episodic content ("clips") can in turn be randomly reassembled and changed by the system. These new clips may also contain fictional experiences. The active system can design new scenarios based on evaluations of the actions carried out (target-oriented/not target-oriented) and the experience stored in the memory and thus look towards the future. If the new fictional content proves useful, it will be consolidated into the memory and thus correspond to real experiences. In the present model, chance is the basis and determining element for the selection and retrieval of memory contents as well as for their reconfiguration. Chance is, if you will, part of the identity of the active system.

The rules of physics apply to both biological systems and artificial intelligences. It has been shown that scope for free decisions and ultimately free will can arise within the framework of these natural laws. Whatever the findings of neuroscience and philosophy, they cannot question the laws of physics and are therefore consistent with the findings that emerge from this model. So free algorithmic decision-making is not fiction and could be applied to machines. Working groups led by Hans Briegel are currently researching how this model might combine with deep learning strategies.

ALGORITHMS AND FREEDOM

Using artificial intelligence to help us search the Internet, drive vehicles, carry out our professional work, etc. is now a daily reality. It is clear that this kind of support also influences our activities. The freedom of our decisions is therefore being influenced by such assistance systems. The question of the extent to which we can still be held responsible for these influenced decisions is currently preoccupying philosophers and lawyers. The simple reasoning involved in the "Trolley Problem" goes to the heart of the dilemma (fig. 2). In the future, assistance systems may make decisions that endanger people's lives in order to save people, and these decisions may go against our own will.

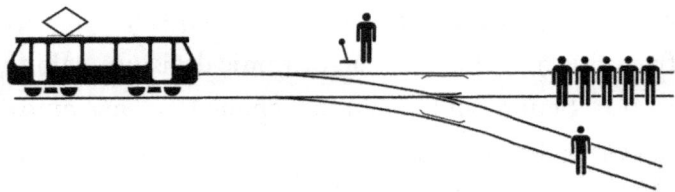

Fig. 2: *The "Trolley Problem." A trolley is moving on a track towards a lever. The person standing by the lever now has two options. 1. He does not act and lets the trolley pass, in which case five people will be run over on the track straight ahead. 2. He pulls the lever and saves the lives of the five people. By pulling the lever, however, the trolley turns into the siding and kills the individual on that track.*[10]

The Trolley Problem is a dramatic representation of a conflict in decision-making. The small everyday decisions that algorithms make for us may not be particularly important when viewed individually, but taken together they can have substantial effects and have a significant impact on our lives. The extent to which these influences are compatible with our free will is the fascinating question that we have to answer.

Notes

1. "De libero arbitrio", Dialogues II, vol. 1/4 in *The Works of Saint Augustine. A Translation for the 21st Century*, 46 vols., John E. Rotelle et al. (eds.) (New York: New City Press, 1991–2019).

2. Hans Helmut Kornhuber and Lüder Deecke, "Hirnpotentialänderungen bei Willkürbewegungen und passiven Bewegungen des Menschen: Bereitschaftspotential und reafferente Potentiale" in *Pflügers Archiv: European Journal of Physiology* 284, 1965, pp. 1–17.

3. Ibid.

4. Benjamin Libet, Curtis A. Gleason, Elwood W. Wright, and Dennis K. Pearl, "Time of conscious intention to act in relation to onset of cerebral activity (readiness-potential): The unconscious initiation of a freely voluntary act" in *Brain* 106, 1983, pp. 623–642.

5. James D. Sauer, Neil Brewer, and Nathan Weber, "Multiple confidence estimates as indices of eyewitness memory" in *Journal of Experimental Psychology: General* 137, 2008, pp. 528–547. doi: 10.1037/a0012712. PMID: 18729714.

6. Veerle Puttemans, Nicole Wenderoth, and Stephan P. Swinnen, "Changes in brain activation during the acquisition of a multifrequency bimanual coordination task: from the cognitive stage to advanced levels of automaticity" in *The Journal of Neuroscience* 25, 2005, pp. 4270–4280. doi: 10.1523/JNEUROSCI.3866-04.2005. PMID: 15858053, PMCID: PMC6725124.

7. Iain McGilchrist, *The Master and His Emissary: The Divided Brain and the Making of the Western World* (London: Yale University Press, 2019).

8. Hans J. Briegel, "On creative machines and the physical origins of freedom" in *Scientific Reports* 2, 2012, p. 522. doi: 10.1038/srep00522. Epub 2012 Jul 20. PMID: 22822427.

9. Francis Crick and Christof Koch, "A framework for consciousness" in *Nature Neuroscience* 6, 2003, pp. 119–126. doi: 10.1038/nn0203-119. PMID: 12555104.

10. https://commons.wikimedia.org/wiki/File:Trolley_Problem.svg (accessed December 12, 2021); https://creativecommons.org/licenses/by-sa/4.0/legalcode (accessed December 12, 2021).

CHAPTER 6

AUTONOMY AND PROTECTION—AMBIVALENCES IN FUNDAMENTAL RIGHTS

STEFAN KORIOTH

I.

"Man is born free, and everywhere he is in chains. Many a one believes himself the master of others, and yet he is a greater slave than they. How has this change come about? I do not know. What can render it legitimate? I believe that I can settle this question."[1] These are the opening sentences of a famous, classic, and still fundamental work on individual and social self-determination and freedom. Rousseau's *Social Contract* addresses the paradox of self-determination and alienation in bourgeois society, the formation of a comprehensive collective will as benefiting freedom, despite the restrictions it imposes on the natural freedom of the individual. Like hardly any other book written in the 18th century, a period characterized by the pathos of freedom, Rousseau carries the reader with him, and at the same time leaves them with many questions. Is man really born free? Is freedom an original gift of every human being that is and must be lost in the process of civilization? Is man really in chains? And if so, who applied the chains? Is it society, is it other individuals—or is it ourselves? Do the chains have to be broken, as Rousseau suggests, or should we accept them in an appropriate form? Under what conditions is giving up natural freedom and engaging in society a benefit?

Fundamental rights, an indispensable part of every modern constitution, are rights to freedom. They presuppose people who are engaged in society. They aim to resolve the major and minor conflicts concerning the exercise of freedom that arise between the bearers of fundamental rights and the public authorities, but also between the subjects of fundamental rights themselves, preferably to maximize freedom. The standards of fundamental rights are the repository of centuries of threats to freedom. Theoretical reflections about freedom, not least Rousseau's, have also been incorporated into current fundamental rights. It is rare that this is explicitly formulated, but it appears in Germany's Basic Law at least in Art. 1, Para. 2: "The German people therefore acknowledge inviolable and inalienable human rights as the basis of every community, of peace and of justice in the world." The implicit, sometimes even unconscious incorporation of ideas about political and philosophical freedom can generally be seen in individual legal arguments and concrete decisions.

To understand the first, basic dimension of fundamental freedom and its protection under current (German) law, we will start by quoting decisions by Germany's Federal Constitutional Court, in clauses that are as succinct as they are demanding: "Fundamental freedom is, from the point of view of the state, formal freedom" and "It is up to the bearer of this freedom whether and how he makes use of his scope for freedom."[2] Accordingly, freedom is the absence of coercion, even going so far as to leave the definition of freedom up to the individual. Specifically, freedom is protected even if its exercise "at least in the eyes of third parties runs counter to the best interests of the bearer of fundamental rights".[3] Moreover, fundamental rights are an offer, not an obligation. They maintain the scope of freedom—a protected legal asset or practice—and the bearer of fundamental rights decides whether and how to make use of it. When the Basic Law was drawn up, the Parliamentary Council initially wanted to formulate Art. 2, Para. 1 of the Basic Law as follows: "Everyone can do and not do what they want." Just because this did not seem serious enough linguistically, it became: "Every person shall have the right to free development of his personality insofar as he does not violate the rights of others or offend against the constitutional order or the moral law."

This is the legal version of what political philosophy calls "negative freedom" —freedom from coercion, individualism, the original freedom that precedes every kind of rule-making. However, the second half of Art. 2, Para. 1 of the Basic Law then goes on to show that things cannot remain this way. The freedom of one individual must be balanced against the freedom of all others and the demands of the common good. When setting limits, however, the individual's exercise of freedom is given particular importance. The exercise of fundamental rights to freedom does not require any justification. The fundamental right guarantees the aspiration that others and the state will in principle refrain from interfering with the exercise of freedom. The necessary limits are subject to the "principle of distribution of the *Rechtsstaat* [rule of law]".⁴ The individual's freedoms are in principle unlimited, and the powers of the state are limited. The state can only restrict freedom if good reasons are given.⁵ The burden of proof for the necessity of encroaching on fundamental rights lies with the state. Conflicts are possible in a number of ways: one person's exercise of freedom can conflict with the freedom of another, whether over the issue of the same fundamental rights or different ones. However, freedom can also conflict with the interests of the common good. The conflict resolution described in the principle of distribution of the *Rechtsstaat* refers to the principle of proportionality, which must be applied in such a way that in principle none of the conflicting legal interests is completely abdicated. It should be possible to reach a sensible balance, a "practical concordance."⁶ "Between the seriousness of the infringement [of freedom] and the importance as well as the urgency of the reasons justifying such infringement, a reasonable balance must still be ensured."⁷ Black-and-white solutions, where in a conflict one legal interest guaranteeing freedom has to withdraw completely in favor of another, is fundamentally excluded by the principle of concordance. This weighing up and assessing in search of a sensible balance is a simple principle that is recognized in the application of fundamental rights. It is therefore all the more surprising that it is occasionally ignored. When the COVID-19 crisis began in March 2020, authorities wanted, among other things, to ban religious gatherings and demonstrations completely and without exception. This complete elimination of fundamental rights was unconstitutional. Of course, in the interest of protecting health, constraints and restrictions might be expected, and it was also possible to prohibit or break up gatherings if these restrictions were not observed—but the general, albeit temporary, exclusion of the exercise of fundamental rights was inadmissible. The courts had to rule on this.[8]

II.

Is a democratic system a guarantee of freedom or can it become a threat to it? First, democracy is freedom's system of government. It enables a society's self-determination through the mutual recognition of its members as equals under the law. Only through this can there be individual and collective autonomy. This applies in any case to all forms of communicative and political freedom; at best the protection of highly personal and individual interests such as life and physical integrity can be achieved outside of democratic forms of decision-making. However, experience shows that even such individual legal interests are always threatened, especially in non-democratic societies.

For Rousseau, the connection between freedom and democracy was clear: natural freedom, the state of nature, had been lost through people's inevitable social engagement. But by working together as members of society with equal rights under the law, people gain collective self-determination, protection, recognition by everyone else, security, and a focus on the common good. For this to happen, procedural rules must be found that enable the common will to develop.

This is on the one hand. But democracy can also become a threat to freedom. The majority principle is a central rule in democratic decision-making. It is this very principle, however, that can lead to the tyranny of the majority, to the outvoting of minorities, and to the abuse of collective freedom of action to the detriment of individual or small groups. There must therefore be rules limiting democratic decision-making; areas that are beyond the control of even the majority must be defined. These areas refer first of all to fundamental rights. The allocation or withholding of freedoms is excluded from majority decision-making in specific situations, and fundamental rights guarantee that one is allowed to deviate from the majority in one's own attitudes and behavior. In fact, these rights are particularly important when it comes to protecting minorities. Religious freedom does not have to be fought for in a society with homogeneity of religion, but it is important and difficult in a multi-faith society when it comes to recognizing religious diversity and minorities. Here and in other constellations where majority and minority are juxtaposed, in the event of conflicting claims to freedom the majority must not take priority because its claims are quantitatively dominant. In a religiously neutral state, for example, a Christian symbol such as a cross is inappropriate in state school classrooms even if a majority of students, parents, and teachers are in favor of it.

The prohibition of outvoting can also be significant in temporal terms. The peaceful use of nuclear energy must face the question of whether today's proponents are allowed to create consequences, for example in the disposal and storage of spent fuel rods, that are irreversible over a period of thousands of years and are left up to the future inhabitants of the planet to deal with. In the context of the current demands for climate protection, the debate about inter-temporal preservation of freedom has become all-pervasive.

Today's freedom may (and perhaps must) be restricted in the interest of future opportunities for the exercise of freedom. Equally, in the case of national debt and social insurance, today's consumption of resources must not deprive future generations of their opportunities. All of this shows that democracy needs scope and limits, as does freedom. Freedom and democracy depend on one another, but they can also threaten one another.

III.

How much state control and regulation does freedom need? This affects other aspects of fundamental rights in addition to the negative, defensive function. First of all, there are freedoms, whose exercise is dependent on rules and laws. This is most evident in the case of property rights. Property and the rights of disposal and exclusivity associated with it are not pre-legal givens such as the rights to life, physical integrity, or conscience. Property is a product of the legal system, as this subject of freedom requires comprehensive regulation. The Constitution's safeguarding of property guarantees the existence of property. Therefore, the legislature may not conclude that it does not have to provide for such a legal institution at all in its legal system. Nevertheless, the law regulates the details, the extent, and the limits of property. The role of regulations is to mediate between various owners, property, and the common good. How a plot of land can be developed doesn't only concern the owner, it also affects the neighbors and the general public.

Another area is more complex and difficult: is it the state's job to guarantee the conditions and opportunities for the exercise of freedom? Is it enough to safeguard the freedom to choose an occupation, or must conditions be created through the education system and practical assistance so that all members of society can actually make use of this freedom? These questions were raised for the first time by socialist theoreticians in the 19th century, who pointed out a blind spot in the old liberal understanding of freedom. They claimed that if the state's role lies exclusively in not interfering with freedom, i.e. protecting it as a "nightwatchman state" by non-action, then everyone is free to sleep under a bridge or in a warm bed at night—the same freedom is indeed not equality in freedom. They said that the state should not ignore the fact that individual requirements for the exercise of freedom are very different—the state must intervene in this respect in a supportive and corrective manner. Purely defensive rights, they concluded, were only of use for the "blessed possessors" [*beati possidentes*]. Completely un-socialist, but in some ways with the same thrust, in the 1920s law theorists first formulated an understanding of freedom and fundamental rights that was not only about defense. They claimed that fundamental rights are not just rights against state interference, but fundamental decisions and values on which a society is united and which it wants to enact and protect. Fundamental rights, they continued, are thus also obligations of the citizen, the tools of the committed citizen—the citizen as opposed to the bourgeois, who only wants to be left in peace. Taking issue with the exclusive classification of basic rights as defensive rights, Rudolf Smend asserted that the rule of law, understood as a system of "apolitical defense and distancing of an internally apolitical and subversive bourgeoisie" did not correspond to the reality of current constitutional law. It was not about the "apolitical wretchedness of a bourgeoisie", but rather the "qualification to be a citizen" that fundamental rights provide. Modern constitutions, he said, want to equip "various parts of the population with freedoms and safeguards, which appear necessary for this group as preconditions of real, not just formal, civic freedom and their empowerment, especially given

Formaldemokratie [a bourgeois notion of democracy in name only]."⁹

Under the Basic Law and with significant support from the Federal Constitutional Court, this view came to full fruition alongside the defensive right in law as a further dimension of fundamental rights. In 1958 the Federal Constitutional Court decreed:

> There is no doubt that the main purpose of basic rights is to protect the individual's sphere of freedom against encroachment by public power: they are the citizen's bulwark against the state. This emerges from both their development as a matter of intellectual history and their adoption into the constitutions of the various states as a matter of political history. [...] But far from being a value-free system the Constitution erects an objective system of values in its section on basic rights, and thus expresses and reinforces the validity of the basic rights. This system of values, centering on the freedom of the human being to develop in society, must apply as a constitutional axiom throughout the whole legal system: it must direct and inform legislation, administration, and judicial decision.¹⁰

Today, in Germany, this is firmly established. But Anglo-Saxon legal systems in particular are more detached from this. In this case, the idea of freedom as the original status of every human being is still central, as it is for the conception of fundamental rights. The fragmentary law can restrict this original freedom if it is in the public interest, in which case, however, the law is actually not obliged to protect freedom but is generally speaking against it. In Germany by contrast—with most continental legal systems now following suit—the state's duties to protect freedom and to create the foundations for the exercise of fundamental rights are derived from the understanding of fundamental rights as basic decisions affecting all areas of life. The result is ambivalent. For the first time in their development, fundamental rights not only draw up the limits of the state, but also form a basis for empowering the activities of public authorities, albeit—and this is the ambivalence—in the sense of protecting the freedom of certain people. In a judgment on climate protection, the Federal Constitutional Court stated that "under certain conditions the Basic Law imposes an obligation to safeguard fundamental freedom over time and to spread the opportunities associated with freedom proportionately across generations." Fundamental rights "as intertemporal guarantees of freedom—afford protection against the greenhouse gas reduction burdens [...] being offloaded unilaterally into the future."[11] Today's freedom may be restricted to the benefit of freedom in the future.

This relatively new development in the centuries-long development of fundamental rights shows that it is a constant and demanding task to harmonize freedom and self-determination with the necessary heteronomy of a social system. Fundamental freedom was never what the author Martin Walser wrote in 1957 as the opinion of a factory owner during the German economic miracle: "At the word freedom, he winced painfully. All against all, he said, that's freedom."[12]

Notes

1. Jean-Jacques Rousseau, *The Social Contract or Principles of Political Right* (1762), trans. H.J. Tozer (London: Wordsworth Editions, 1998), p. 5.

2. Decision of the Federal Constitutional Court, BVerfGE 102, 370 (395).

3. Decision of the Federal Constitutional Court, BVerfGE 128, 282 (304).

4. Carl Schmitt, *Constitutional Theory*, trans. Jeffrey Seitzer (Durham NC: Duke University Press, 2008), p. 170.

5. For example, Decision of the Federal Constitutional Court, BVerfGE 128, 226 (244 f.).

6. Konrad Hesse, *Grundzüge des Verfassungsrechts*, 20th edn. (Heidelberg 1995), note 317 ff.

7. Decision of the Federal Constitutional Court, BVerfGE 67, 167 (178).

8. Federal Constitutional Court, April 15, 2020, Judgment of the 1st Chamber of the Second Senate (1 BvR 828/20), *Neue Juristische Wochenschrift* (2020), 1426.

9. Rudolf Smend, "Bürger und Bourgeois im deutschen Staatsrecht" (1933), in Rudolf Smend, *Staatsrechtliche Abhandlungen und andere Aufsätze*, 2nd edn., (Berlin, 1968), pp. 309 ff., 314f., 317, 319.

10. Decision of the Federal Constitutional Court, BVerfGE 7, 198 (205). See https://germanlawarchive.iuscomp.org/?p=51 (accessed November 30, 2021).

11. Order of the Federal Constitutional Court, March 24, 2021 - 1 BvR 2656/18, headnote 4. https://www.bundesverfassungsgericht.de/SharedDocs/Entscheidungen/EN/2021/03/rs20210324_1bvr265618en.html (accessed November 30, 2021).

12. Martin Walser, *Ehen in Philippsburg* [1957] (Frankfurt: Suhrkamp, 2004), p. 76 [*The Gadarene Club*, trans. Eva Figes (London: Longmans, 1960)].

CHAPTER 7

SUSTAINABILITY AS A PREREQUISITE OF PERSONAL AND ENTREPRENEURIAL FREEDOM

HILDEGARD WORTMANN

"A fundamental turning point in a company's relationship with individuals and with its economic and social environment." This is how the prestigious *Gabler Wirtschaftslexikon* defines the term "transformation,"[1] a term that has long been part of everyday language for us all. And rightly so, because one thing's for sure, the transformation that we are currently experiencing is indeed "fundamental" and it is accelerating exponentially, not least as a result of the COVID-19 pandemic. More than ever, people care about the world they live in, because of the vulnerability that the virus has revealed to us, but much more and more basically because of the epochal challenges we are facing due to climate change.

As a result, in December 2015, almost 190 global partners signed up to the Paris Climate Agreement, which said that global warming should be kept well below 2°C, and that temperature rises were to be limited to 1.5°C through additional measures.[2] Six years later, in October 2021, the sixth and latest report by the Intergovernmental Panel on Climate Change (IPCC) presents a sobering analysis: "Global surface temperature will continue to increase until at least the mid-century under all emissions scenarios considered. Global warming of 1.5°C and 2°C will be exceeded during the 21st century unless deep reductions in carbon dioxide (CO_2) and other greenhouse gas emissions occur in the coming decades."[3] The message is unequivocal: climate protection can no longer be delayed. The overwhelming majority of people in our part of the world agree. According to an EU Eurobarometer survey published in July 2021, "European citizens believe climate change is the single most serious problem facing the world. More than nine out of ten people surveyed consider climate change to be a serious problem (93 percent), with almost eight out of ten (78 percent) considering it to be very serious."[4] Frans Timmermans, EU Commission Vice-President responsible for the European Green Deal, said: "Europeans recognize the long-term risks posed by the climate and biodiversity crises, and expect industry, governments, and the European Union to take action."[5]

The citizen and youth movements that are fighting for more climate protection are now operating worldwide. They are an expression of the younger generation's justified demand for sustainable visions of the future. And they are getting impatient, as the statements issued by "Fridays for Future" demonstrate: "Why should we build for a future that will soon no longer be worth living? Our answer to this question is the climate strike: we are striking for an effective policy that does justice to the extent of the climate crisis. We have ten years to reach our goals and we must start now. Let's act!"[6]

What does this mean for us in the automotive industry? It means we have to take responsibility. We have to act now instead of waiting. We must stand up for what we believe in. This is what the millennial generation expects from companies—and even more urgently the generation of those born in the 21st century who have been dubbed "Generation Z" or "Generation C." The standard interpretation is that

"C" stands for "Connection",[7] namely the fact that this generation grew up with digital communications practically from childhood. I would go further and say that "C" stands for Creation, Curation, Community, and for Connection—that is, for Creativity, for Connectivity, and for Community spirit as well as for Care and responsibility, which is one way of interpreting Curation. Today this "Generation C" already comprises over a quarter of the global population; in 2025 this will be more than 45 percent of all potential car buyers. They are rightly demanding products and entrepreneurial action that match their personal values in terms of ecological goals, social responsibility—not least with a view to all-embracing diversity—and honest business management. Studies of changes in consumer behavior confirm this in many cases. In Germany, the COVID-19 pandemic has accelerated not just the digitalization of retail but also consumers' desire for more sustainability. In a survey, almost half of the respondents (49 percent) stated that sustainability is important to them when buying clothes.[8] And in the food sector, the GfK Consumer Confidence Barometer said as early as 2014 that more than half of consumers explicitly preferred products that are sustainable and regional.[9] Sustainability has become a decisive purchasing criterion. Purchasing decisions are becoming statements.

SUSTAINABILITY AND FREEDOM

I would like to go one more important step further. I am convinced that sustainability is a prerequisite of freedom. Sustainability and freedom are not contradictory, but are mutually interdependent, because we can only live in freedom in a sustainable world. At the Convoco Forum on July 31, 2021, I put it this way: "For me, maintaining individual and sustainable mobility is a great asset to personal freedom, independence, and self-determination—not a conflict."[10]

In this I am echoing the political scientist Claus Leggewie, who warned in an interview: "A free society that is not sustainable undermines its own means of existence; a society that aspires to sustainability must not allow restrictions to such an extent that people become unfree." And when asked "What can the individual do to reconcile freedom and sustainability?" he replied, "We have to learn to think in the future perfect: by the years 2030, 2050, or 2100 what are we likely to have done in order to be able to live sustainably? This translates the scope for freedom in temporal terms into a generational relationship that avoids thinking purely in the here and now. Of course, new freedoms will also be opened up by voluntarily forgoing options such as rapid consumption and free time, because freedom in the present ends where freedom in the future begins."[11] This in turn recalls Immanuel Kant: "No one can compel me to be happy in accordance with his conception of the welfare of others, for each may seek his happiness in whatever way he sees fit, so long as he does not infringe upon the freedom of others to pursue a similar end."[12] In short, Kant says that the freedom of one individual ends where the freedom of another begins. And like Aristotle and Thomas Hobbes before him, Kant also distinguishes between positive and negative freedom, that is, freedom *to* and freedom *from*.

But how do we understand freedom today? It is evidently a commodity that is increasing in value, as a study in Germany shows: 10 percent more people than of those surveyed in 2012 agree with the statement "All of us are the state, and Germany's development lies with us as citizens." Equally, opinions on the extent to which an individual has an influence have changed. When asked, "As a citizen, do you have any influence on what happens locally, or are you powerless in that respect?" 47 percent of those polled answered positively; in 1992 only 22 percent thought they did. And another survey result shows that the willingness to get involved in society has also increased.[13]

Let's look more closely at the economy. More and more companies are providing encouraging examples of positive entrepreneurial freedom, that is freedom *to*. One example is the Danish energy company Ørsted, which has transformed from an oil and gas company into the largest offshore wind farm company in Scandinavia.[14] Or the French cosmetics company L'Oréal, which has reduced its CO_2 emissions by 80 percent since 2005 and its water consumption by 50 percent. Alexandra Palt, the Austrian Chief Sustainability Officer at L'Oréal (and former equal opportunities activist), says: "Our philosophy with regard to investors and the stock market, to our consumers and all our employees is that we want to combine sustainability, profit, and high productivity."[15] In Germany, meanwhile, almost 70 companies and corporations, from Adidas, Hermes, and Miele to Schwäbisch-Hall and Vattenfall, have joined together to found the initiative Stiftung 2º – German Businesses for Climate Protection Now. Their program begins as follows: "Climate change has become tangible for all of us. The latest report by the Intergovernmental Panel on Climate Change (IPCC) makes it unmistakably clear that there is no more time to lose in taking decisive action to counter global warming."[16]

POLITICAL FRAMEWORKS

We're also talking about freedom when we talk about mobility. Since COVID-19 in particular, we have become very aware of the enormous value of personal mobility. Personal mobility means freedom, self-determination, and independence. The task now is to make personal mobility sustainable. The job of business is to develop products and services that give people the freedom to live sustainably and that contribute to a better life. If that succeeds, sustainability does not mean forgoing anything. Here's Claus Leggewie again: "A society that aspires to sustainability must not allow restrictions to such an extent that people become unfree."[17] Politicians should focus on this—in the case of the EU Green Deal as well as in the plans drawn up by US President Joe Biden's administration for a significant acceleration in climate protection.

For the automotive industry, the roadmap towards sustainable personal mobility has already been drawn up. By far the most efficient and uncompromising way of achieving decarbonization and a better future is electromobility. That is why, for us at Audi, the future of mobility is electric. Every new Audi model that comes onto the market from 2026 will be fully electric. But that's not enough. An accelerated expansion of renewable energies and an even faster expansion of the charging infrastructure are urgently required. We need effective cooperation between politics, business, and society to meet the challenges. It is important to break new ground and recognize the challenges as opportunities, not as threats. We have to develop convincing perspectives with new strength for the future. Visions create identification and a willingness to change, ideally with an enthusiasm that inspires all citizens and every company—especially in the post-COVID-19 era.

And we need international cooperation, now more than ever. Stefan Oschmann wrote in the 2021 Convoco Edition, considering the lessons of the pandemic: "…We now have unprecedented access to progress made around the world in technology and research. This also improves our lives. Thus, we ultimately benefit when the global community moves closer together."[18] And on the subject of Europe he adds: "Now is a time when the EU can create positive impetus and provide a convincing model of how value-based international cooperation can work."[19]

LIVING DIGITAL TRANSFORMATION

We should heed the call to take a bold approach to digitalization instead of being afraid of new technologies.[20] It is important to network the physical and digital worlds—to create a "phygital" world. We need to combine supply, trade, and customers across all industries, and improve products and services in such a way that creates permanent added value for customers. To do this, digitalization and sustainability go hand in hand, also when it comes to the resource-efficient optimization of production and logistics. Keeping an eye on the entire value chain is one of the principles of a holistic approach to sustainability.

Anyone who has ever dealt with public authorities in a convenient and paperless way online has seen that sustainable digitalization creates freedom. With the help of cloud technologies, employees are going about their digitalized daily working life flexibly and independently of their location, as it is possible to view and edit important data from any device. Or let's take a look at China, where almost all areas of life have been digitalized through the WeChat app. Users can order a taxi, pay their electricity bills, search for people nearby, or book doctor's appointments—all centrally via an app. In the case of mobility, another game-changer will be the driverless car of the future: highly automated driving will transform the car into a completely new living space, a place that will give us a whole new level of freedom—the freedom to organize the time of a car journey individually and freely.

Last but not least, digital champions, i.e. companies with an extremely high level of digitalization, prove that digitalization pays off. For example, a study in Germany showed that 81 percent of these companies are coping well with the COVID-19 crisis because they had already extensively digitalized their business model or their processes.[21] Even after the pandemic, these digital leaders see themselves as ideally positioned: with the help of digital solutions they can further increase their sales, turnover, and product and service quality. According to the study, "41 percent of companies are increasingly using digital platforms such as comparison and rating portals, search engines, sharing platforms, app stores, and online marketplaces. Companies use digital channels and social networks to market products and services. They communicate the latest offers online or advise their customers online via video. A stable and secure network infrastructure is therefore required."[22] A swift, accelerated expansion of network coverage and the rapid introduction of 5G technology are essential for this, because manufacturing and production facilities can also benefit from digital transformation. In Industry 4.0, we are already seeing automated processes controlled by artificial intelligence and the extensive networking of machines.

CONCLUSION

My personal conclusion is that our vision of the future is hopeful and optimistic. My entrepreneurial goal is to make a contribution to a better, more livable future. If we exploit the great potential offered by the transformation we defined at the beginning as a "fundamental turning point", we will contribute to a better world, because sustainable corporate management means freedom. Speaking for the automotive industry, maintaining personal and sustainable mobility is a great asset to individual freedom, independence, and self-determination—not a conflict. In short, sustainability is the new premium. We have to take responsibility for shaping the future, that is conserve our natural resources, stop climate change, create modern types of employment, and use significant technologies that make our society more humane and more resilient.

Notes

1. Gabler Wirtschaftslexikon online, *Business Transformation*, https://wirtschaftslexikon.gabler.de/definition/business-transformation-51893: "Eine fundamentale Wende in der Beziehung eines Unternehmens zu Einzelpersonen und zu seinem wirtschaftlichen und gesellschaftlichen Umfeld" (accessed November 11, 2021).

2. European Commission, Paris Agreement, https://ec.europa.eu/clima/eu-action/international-action-climate-change/climate-negotiations/paris-agreement_en (accessed November 1, 2021). The Agreement was formally ratified by the EU on October 5, 2016.

3. IPCC, *Sixth Assessment Report* (AR6). Working Group I: The Physical Science Basis, https://www.ipcc.ch/report/ar6/wg1/downloads/report/IPCC_AR6_WGI_Headline_Statements.pdf, p. 1 (accessed November 1, 2021).

4. European Commission, "Eurobarometer Survey: Europeans consider climate change to be the most serious problem facing the world" Press release, July 5, 2021, https://ec.europa.eu/commission/presscorner/detail/en/ip_21_3156 (accessed November 1, 2021).

5. Ibid.

6. Fridays for Future, https://fridaysforfuture.de/ (accessed November 1, 2021).

7. For example: FOCUS online, "Kennen Sie die Generation C?", 2.7.2019, https://www.focus.de/finanzen/boerse/fazit-kennen-sie-die-generation-c_id_10886240.html (accessed November 1, 2021).

8. IFH Köln, *Nachhaltigkeit in der amazonisierten Welt*, July 2021, https://www.ifhkoeln.de/produkt/nachhaltigkeit-in-der-amazonisierten-welt/ (accessed November 1, 2021).

9. GfK, *Nachhaltig oder regional? Am besten beides*, Consumer Index 03/2014, https://www.nim.org/sites/default/files/medien/1/dokumente/gfk_consumer_index_032014.pdf (accessed November 1, 2021).

10. Hildegard Wortmann, Convoco Forum 2021, https://www.youtube.com/watch?v=mUd69B9VJzw (accessed November 1, 2021).

11. Pax-Bank, *Drei Fragen an Claus Leggewie: die Freiheit zum Verzicht*, Pax-Bank Note, 2nd quarter, 2018, https://www.pax-bank.de/content/dam/f0395-0/interneinhalte/pdf/paxbanknote/2018-PBN/PBN_2018_02.pdf, p. 5 (accessed November 1, 2021).

12. Immanuel Kant, "Theory and Practice II" in *Political Writings*, ed. H.S. Reiss, trans. H.B. Nisbet (Cambridge: CUP, 1970), p. 74.

13. Ulrike Ackermann (ed.), *Freiheitsindex Deutschland 2017* (Frankfurt: Humanities Online, 2017).

14. See Hildegard Wortmann, "Vorsprung ist der Erfolg von morgen" in *Handelsblatt*, July 12, 2021 https://www.handelsblatt.com/meinung/gastbeitraege/gastkommentar-vorsprung-ist-der-erfolg-von-morgen/27406530.html (accessed November 1, 2021).

15. Laura Cwiertina and Uwe Jean Heuser interview with Alexandra Palt, "Warum nicht jetzt, Frau Palt?" in *Zeit Online*, October 6, 2021 https://www.zeit.de/2021/41/alexandra-palt-klimawandel-l-oreal-nachhaltigkeit-unternehmen-greenwashing/seite-2?utm_referrer=https%3A%2F%2Fwww.google.com%2F (accessed November 1, 2021).

16. Stiftung 2° – German Businesses for Climate Protection, *An Implementation Programme for Climate Neutrality. Now*, October 11, 2021 https://klimawirtschaft.org/en/implementation-programme-climate-neutrality-7249 (accessed November 1, 2021).

17. See Pax-Bank, *Drei Fragen an Claus Leggewie.*

18. Stefan Oschmann, "Collaboration Strengthens the Immune System of the Global Community" in Corinne Michaela Flick (ed.), *New Global Alliances: Institutions, Alignments, and Legitimacy in the Contemporary World* (Munich: Convoco Foundation, 2021), p. 157.

19. Oschmann, "Collaboration Strengthens the Immune System of the Global Community," p. 161.

20. Cf. Wortmann, "Vorsprung ist der Erfolg von morgen."

21. Digitalisierungsindex, Small and medium-sized businesses 2020/21 https://www.digitalisierungsindex.de/aktuelle-studie/ (accessed November 1, 2021).

22. Karoline Bergmann, "Digitization index for businesses: Corona accelerates digitization in medium-sized businesses" in *Telekom*, December 2, 2020, https://www.telekom.com/en/media/media-information/archive/digitization-index-for-businesses-corona-accelerates-digitization-in-medium-sized-businesses-613546 (accessed November 1, 2021).

CHAPTER 8

FREEDOM AND THE TENSIONS BETWEEN COLLECTIVE VALUES: A HISTORICAL PERSPECTIVE ON THE 19th CENTURY

JÖRN LEONHARD

In his novel, *The Magic Mountain*, Thomas Mann was looking back at the 19th century as he described an argument about which lines of tradition had created Europe—a Europe that for Mann had become ancient history as a result of World War I. While the Italian Ludovico Settembrini represents the pioneer of civil liberties in the fight against retrograde forces, championing rational optimism and an unwavering idea of progress, his opponent Leo Naphta embodies the

Jesuits, communistic apocalypse, and the subordination of individual freedom to radical ideas of community and hierarchy. This at first glance apparently contradictory mixture of characteristics reveals something about the upheaval in ideological certainties that took place in the early 20th century. Settembrini expresses his belief in Europe's progressive history, which for him, as a representative of liberalism, was based on the ever-widening scope of freedom that began with the Renaissance, and without which neither Humanism, morality, the Enlightenment, the bourgeois revolutions since 1789, nor the modern state could have existed. Naphta counters that "your great heroic age" is a thing of the past. Future revolutions, he says, have nothing to do with liberal ideals and the fight for greater freedom; rather, they will be based on discipline, sacrifice, and the renunciation of the ego. For any human being, he continues, bourgeois freedom and humanistic justice can only mean paralyzing weakness and leveling out all oppositions. One was "'just' according to one standard *or* according to the other. All the rest was liberalism—in which nobody nowadays took any stock."[1]

In this debate, which runs through much of Mann's *Bildungsroman*, the controversy about the value of freedom plays an important role. A glance at the 19th century shows that ideas about freedom were changing in a powerful way and varied greatly between different societies. After the revolutions in North America in 1776 and in France in 1789, it became paradigmatic that freedom could not represent a value that was independent of other political and social objectives. This constellation of competition and complementariness gave rise to polarities, especially between freedom and equality or between freedom and security, polarities that already existed in the 19th century and which have continued to assert their relevance up to the present day.

The expectations associated with the concept of freedom were powerful and dynamic, not least because the experiences of revolution that had taken place after the last third of the 18th century could not be contained, continuing to have an effect well beyond 1799 and 1815. Jacob Burckhardt summed it up in 1871, saying "that actually everything up to today is nothing but the age of revolution." In the "great drama" of the historical upheavals since 1789, Burckhardt recognized "one movement which is antithetical to all the known past of our globe."[2] In this, the concept of revolution became detached from its focus on a selectively defined historical event and became a hallmark of the era itself. The concept no longer contained the idea of disempowering a given political and social order over a period of time. The return to a *status quo ante* by way of a restoration, which was so passionately discussed after Napoleon's defeat in 1814/15, seemed impossible.³

With the invention of "revolution" as an epochal term, post-1814/15 commentators also reflected a fundamental upheaval in the understanding of freedom since the last third of the 18th century. They located themselves in their own post-revolutionary present, in which the revolution could only be sublated dialectically and no longer pursued in the form of a restoration. In this sense, an end to the revolution was no longer conceivable. Rather, every present day was a period of accelerated transition and ongoing crisis, and it was against this background that the understanding of freedom had to be continually redefined. As the conflicts that had broken out in 1789 continued in a new guise and with changed forms and constellations, confidence in a long-term, stable regulatory framework for politics and society diminished. In 1850 the French commentator and political theorist Alexis de Tocqueville summed up this reduced predictability: "What I see clearly is, that for sixty years we have been deceiving ourselves by imagining that we saw the end of the Revolution. [...] It is now evident that the tide is rising, [...]; that not only we have not seen the end of the stupendous revolution which began before our day, but that the infant just born will scarcely see it." He continues that "society is not in the process of modification, but of transformation" and that this is responsible for these long-term effects.[4] The main theme of Tocqueville's thinking was not just the investigation of the structural causes of the French Revolution and its continuing shock waves up to his own time, but beginning with his fundamental 1835 work on democracy in America he questioned the conditions under which liberty and equality might coexist.

These early diagnoses indicate that 19th-century commentators were trying repeatedly to pin down the changing understanding of freedom in relation to other value concepts. In this respect, the triad of "liberty, equality, and fraternity," vigorously advocated by the French revolutionaries, already contained moments of tension. "Liberté" relied primarily on a justification in natural law, on the ideal of a politically liberated civil society, and the fight against irrational bonds, feudal relics, and corporate privileges in an estate-based society. However, this did not yet answer the question of what qualifications are required to exercise civil liberties, which hinted at the conflicts over whether property or education were a precondition, conflicts that would soon develop. "Égalité," on the other hand, referred to different expectations of the future, depending on whether its proponents backed legal, political/constitutional, or extensive social equality. Conflicting concepts of revolution developed in line with these differing orientations, focusing on the fight for civil equality under the law, for political civil liberties in a constitution, or based on the belief in social revolutionary violence. Lastly, commentators could relate "Fraternité" to the idea of the nation and the sovereignty of the people, but also to the idea of international solidarity among all free nations.

Compared with France, the British-born understanding of freedom in the 19th century seemed to be characterized by a distinctive continuity of the unwritten constitution and a seemingly organic development of the constitution without revolutionary ruptures.[5] This difference between revolutionary upheavals in continental European societies and the continuity of the English *ancien régime* alongside evolutionary reform became a leitmotif in the interpretation of British history after the 17th century—and indeed was already taken up by British historians of Victorianism such as Thomas B. Macaulay. This was the "Whig interpretation of history," which characterized history since the 17th century as a continuous and successful struggle against absolutist tendencies and towards ever-greater civil liberties. Accordingly, the national self-image that emerged from this in contradistinction to continental Europe appealed to "liberties, parliament and Protestantism."

The main point of the "Whig interpretation of history" was to emphasize the long duration of the English *ancien régime* since the crises of the 17th century.[6] In contrast to the negative conception of the *ancien régime* in continental Europe which had been formed during the French Revolution, from the perspective of English history the concept highlighted a decisive advantage in the English history of freedom, a concept that drew on the outcome of the crises in the 17th century and could be combined with the arguments of classical republicanism.[7] The growth of parliamentary sovereignty over history, aristocratic parliamentary parties, the uncodified nature of the constitution, and the legal practice of "common law" were, according to this view, decisive outcomes of conflicts in the 17th century or were historically established during this period.[8] This created the ideal image of an incremental adjustment of the system based on gradual improvements to changed political, economic, and social conditions. After 1789 above all, this could be contrasted meaningfully with the revolutionary upheavals that were taking place in the name of abstract principles. In the wars against Napoleon in particular, recourse to constitutional practice and the traditions of freedom contained within it also served as a decisive resource for formulating the image of the British nation that was to unite the English, Welsh, Scots, and Irish.

As the 19th century progressed, the different characteristics of freedom amid the tensions posed by other collective values became more pronounced. First, freedom could be applied to international relations between states to express independence and equality externally and influence the development of international law on that basis. Second, against the background of the state's gradual advance and an expansion of nation states and empires, a functional differentiation of civil, political/constitutional, social, and economic concepts of freedom and their respective demands emerged. Third, the scope for individuals' self-realization became the subject of new forms of debate and processes of negotiation. This is precisely where we can locate the polarities of the concept of freedom in relation to other values. The formation of nations, the internal differentiation of statehood, and the dynamics of social developments meant that the possibilities and limits of freedom had to be constantly renegotiated in multiple areas of tension. But these tensions should not be understood from the outset as an opposition between fundamentally incompatible values. Rather, complementary processes and complex interdependencies emerged. Four of them are outlined here through typical examples.

(1) Freedom and equality. Both concepts and the relationship between them were part of the canon of modern revolutions from 1776/89 until 1917. In practice, however, the waves of revolution in Europe and especially events in France post 1815 showed how specific tensions between freedom and equality developed. The monarchical experiments that created a limited concept of political freedom under the constitutional monarchy after 1814/15 and in favor of the wealthy mercantile middle classes after the July Revolution of 1830 resulted in instability. In February 1848, another version of the constitutional monarchy in France offered no further option for creating a contemporary, liberal system. While in France the struggle over the structure of the social republic and with it the structure and scope of social equality soon came to a head, in Germany the model of the constitutional state with a monarch at its head took control as a way of realizing political civil liberties in an as yet

non-unified nation state. In other European contexts as well, such as in Belgium as early as 1830 and in the Kingdom of Piedmont-Sardinia after 1848, constitutional monarchy was the preferred model for civil liberties to the exclusion of social-revolutionary ideas of equality.

In France things were completely different. The constitution of the Second Republic of 1848 with its emphasis on democratic male suffrage appears in the sequence of constitutions since 1789 as a democratic episode between the July Monarchy, the presidential constitution of 1848, and the Second Empire of Napoleon III. It was based on the republican constitution of 1793, with its emphasis on popular sovereignty, the right to resist, basic social rights, and a unicameral parliament, and was combined with a strict separation of powers and a strong, directly elected president. The prohibition of re-election led to the *coup d'état* of Napoleon's nephew, Louis Bonaparte, in 1851, which was caused by a mixture of social polarization, fear of revolution, and a Bonapartist politics of the past. The fact that constitutions, as guarantors of political freedom, could not curb the momentum of political upheaval and social movements seemed to be immediately apparent in the case of France. Karl Marx's famous analysis in his essay on the *18th Brumaire of Louis Bonaparte* bears witness to this.[9]

Even for contemporary commentators, the notion that a new post-revolutionary justification for political rule had come into effect with the reign of Napoleon III had implications far beyond the French domestic context.[10]

Napoleon III's rulership represented a particular challenge for critical observers such as Alexis de Tocqueville. He saw Napoleon III's activities as threatening to undermine freedom through deliberate promises of equality. Napoleon's appeals to the idea of equality in the sovereignty of the people served such a purpose, as did his use of plebiscites to guarantee the transition to a presidential dictatorship after 1849. Behind the facade of equality, however, the state executive became independent. Similar tendencies, the call for more equality while simultaneously eroding civil liberties, were identified by contemporary commentators in other "white revolutionaries" such as Camillo di Cavour in Piedmont-Sardinia and Otto von Bismarck in Prussia.

(2) Freedom and unity. The new ideal of the nation state as the guarantor of territorial sovereignty abroad and of integration at home emerged in the 19th century. On the one hand, the homogenizing nation state, with its tools such as the right to vote, compulsory military service, and compulsory education, promised to act as

a framework for progress, as a guarantor of civil liberties. On the other hand, the nation as a superior value could be used against the freedom of the individual. In this spirit, invoking the national community, where civil liberties should take a back seat in favor of the nation, reflected the critique of society as the mere sum of individual egoistical interests.

(3) Freedom and security. With the external and internal expansion of the modern state came specific promises of order and stability. They were not least a reaction to experiences of revolution and the threats they posed. For Germany in particular, citing the example of social revolutionary violence in France after 1792 played a decisive role. From this perspective, freedom always seemed in danger of spilling over into uncontrolled chaos and violence, thereby devaluing demands that were in themselves legitimate. Security as the opposite of freedom that had been construed too broadly became more important in tandem with the argument that security was a bulwark against revolution, for example after 1814/15, after 1830, and after 1848. In addition, the intensifying international competition between states and the emergence of Social Darwinism in the 1870s—the idea of a permanent struggle for each nation's own future

viability—reinforced the perception of a polarity between freedom and security. On the other hand, for the first time, stability and order appeared as the kind of conditions that enhanced predictability and without which civil liberties could not be imagined.

(4) Freedom and state intervention. This last polarity was closely linked to the change in the notion of statehood that took place in the 19th century. The idea of an active role for the state in implementing social welfare, the organization of public services as in the case of Bismarck's social policy in the German Empire after 1871, undoubtedly represented social progress. But it was also intended as a strategy of political disenfranchisement and as a bulwark against revolution, which in the case of Germany explained the juxtaposition of the political repression of social democracy and the promise of security created by the state. This tension, which was only suggested at the time, gathered pace in the early 20th century, after which civil liberties were restricted to the maximum extent during the world wars, the latter becoming efficiency tests for the survival of states, nations, and empires. The concepts of "organized capitalism", "state socialism," and the "national community" which were developed after 1914 referred to the supremacy of the state and

a possible suspension of individual civil liberties.[11] In the long term, many notions of social engineering and the euphoria of state-centered planning drew on such approaches and experiences of state intervention. Despite all their differences, this is what connected the neo-corporatism of Italian fascism as an expression of the *stato totalitario*, the American New Deal as an answer to the dual crisis of democracy and capitalism post 1929, the Swedish ideal of *Folkhemmet*, and the social policy of National Socialism.[12]

Attentive 19th-century commentators were immediately aware of the tensions between freedom and other collective values, indeed it acted as a powerful motor for the development of political theories. Two of the best-known examples in this context are the thoughts of Alexis de Tocqueville in his 1835 analysis *Democracy in America* and John Stuart Mill's 1859 essay *On Liberty*. Tocqueville noted a widespread similarity of living conditions in the United States. Above all, he referred to the local community as the people's "school" of freedom,[13] as counterbalancing the centralized state, and as being characterized by short electoral periods, a free press, diverse opinion forming, and socialization through clubs and religious communities. As a result, according to Tocqueville, habits (*mœurs*) were formed that went beyond mere institutions and allowed the habitual practice and concrete experience of freedom and equality. For Tocqueville, freedom in a largely equal society such as that of North America was threatened by three tendencies. First, a threat was posed by the majority. Protection of minorities therefore seemed to him to be just as fundamental as a system of institutional checks and balances for decentralizing power to communities, associations, courts, the local newspapers, and the free exercise of religion. In all this, Tocqueville was also positing an alternative to Napoleon III's Second Empire. Second, the concentration on purely individual freedom, the retreat into the private sphere, and the focus on maximizing economic profit brought about a gradual depoliticization through the seductive despotism of the authorities. Third, Tocqueville noted a mediocrity in cultural and scientific achievements as a result of the far-reaching influence of judicial power on US political life.[13]

In his essay *On Liberty*, John Stuart Mill also emphasized the threat to freedom posed by the tyranny of the majority. This must be counteracted, he wrote, by protecting freedom of expression, of thought, and of assembly, as well as freedom of lifestyle. Above all, however, he pointed out that freedom should not be played off against other collective values. Rather, the individual exercise of civil liberties benefits society as a whole—arguments are constantly tested, compromises are reached, and finding consensus in debate is also important. Mill vehemently opposed philanthropic notions of equality, writing that only inequality and competition force political, social, and cultural systems to adapt, thus creating the decisive prerequisite for progress and prosperity.[14]

The global pandemic is not the only time the tensions between freedom and equality and between freedom and security or health have been re-assessed. A look back at the long 19th century shows us not merely the range of various notions of freedom as they have been differentiated temporally, spatially, and in terms of function. Above all, it points out that the definition of freedom has always included polarity and being interwoven with other value concepts. The latter formed and still form the basis of how concepts of freedom develop, how they are challenged, adapted, and redefined.

Notes

1. Thomas Mann, *The Magic Mountain*, trans. H.T. Lowe-Porter (Harmondsworth: Penguin, 1980) pp. 400, 691.
2. Jacob Burkhardt, *Judgements on History and Historians* (Oxford: Routledge Classics, 2007), p. 245.

3. Panajotis Kondylis, "Reaktion, Restauration" in Otto Brunner, Werner Conze, and Reinhart Koselleck (eds.), *Geschichtliche Grundbegriffe. Historisches Lexikon zur politisch-sozialen Sprache in Deutschland*, vol. 5 (Stuttgart: Klett-Cotta Verlag, 1984), pp. 179–230, here p. 197.

4. "Ce qui est clair pour moi, c'est qu'on s'est trompé depuis soixante ans en croyant voir le but de la révolution ... Il est évident que le flot continue à marcher ... que non-seulement nous n'avons pas vu la fin de l'immense révolution qui a commencé avant nous, mais que l'enfant qui naît aujourd'hui ne la verra vraisemblablement pas." Alexis de Tocqueville, *Letter to Eugène Stoffels*, April 28, 1850 in *Memoirs, Letters, and Remains of Alexis de Tocqueville* (Cambridge and London: Macmillan, 1861), vol. 1, p. 423.

5. Michael Foley, *The Politics of the British Constitution* (Manchester: Manchester University Press, 1999); Jörn Leonhard, "Die Grammatik der Gesellschaft: Perspektiven der Verfassungsgeschichten in Frankreich und Großbritannien seit dem 19. Jahrhundert" in *Der Staat. Zeitschrift für Staatslehre und Verfassungsgeschichte, deutsches und europäisches öffentliches Recht*, supplement 18: "Verfassungsgeschichte in Europa," ed. Helmut Neuhaus (Berlin: Duncker & Humblot, 2010,) pp. 49–70.

6. J.C.D. Clark, *English Society 1688–1832. Ideology, Social Structure and Political Practice during the Ancien Régime* (Cambridge: Cambridge University Press, 1985); Glenn Burgess, *The Politics of the Ancient Constitution: An Introduction to English Political Thought, 1603–1642* (Basingstoke: Macmillan, 1992).

7. J.G.A. Pocock, *The Ancient Constitution and the Feudal Law: A Study of English Historical Thought in the Seventeenth Century* (Cambridge: Cambridge University Press, 1957).

8. Ronald G. Asch, "Das Common Law als Sprache und Norm der politischen Kommunikation in England" in Heinz Duchhardt and Gert Melville (eds.), *Im Spannungsfeld von*

Recht und Ritual. Soziale Kommunikation in Mittelalter und Früher Neuzeit (Cologne: Böhlau, 1997), pp. 103–136.

9. Karl Marx, *The Eighteenth Brumaire of Louis Bonaparte* (New York: Cosimo Classics, 2008).

10. Melvin Richter, "A Family of Political Concepts: Tyranny, Despotism, Bonapartism, Caesarism, Dictatorship, 1750–1917" in *European Journal of Political Theory* 4/3, 2005, pp. 221–249; Jörn Leonhard, "Das Präsens der Revolution: Der Bonapartismus in der europäischen Geschichte des 19. und 20. Jahrhunderts" in Werner Daum, Kathrin S. Hartmann, Simon Palaoro, and Bärbel Suderbrink (eds.), *Kommunikation und Konfliktaustrag. Verfassungskultur als Faktor politischer und gesellschaftlicher Machtverhältnisse* (Berlin: Berliner Wissenschaftsverlag, 2010), pp. 293–317.

11. Jörn Leonhard, *Pandora's Box: A History of the First World War*, trans. Patrick Camiller (Cambridge, MA/London: The Belknap Press of Harvard University Press, 2018), pp. 182–210, 677–685.

12. Kiran Klaus Patel, *The New Deal. A Global History* (Princeton: Princeton University Press, 2016).

13. Alexis de Tocqueville, *Democracy in America*, vols. 1 and 2, trans. Henry Reeve, the Pennsylvania State University, Electronic Classics Series, http://seas3.elte.hu/coursematerial/LojkoMiklos/Alexis-de-Tocqueville-Democracy-in-America.pdf, p. 78 (accessed January 21, 2022).

14. Tocqueville, *Democracy in America*.

15. J.S. Mill, *'On Liberty' and Other Writings*, ed. Stefan Collini (Cambridge: Cambridge University Press, 1989).

CHAPTER 9

INDIVIDUAL AND SOCIAL DIMENSIONS OF FREEDOM AND LIBERTY

BIRKE HÄCKER

INTRODUCTORY REMARKS

What is "freedom"? And how much of it do we have to forgo in order to be truly "free"? To get to the bottom of the second question, a question that appears paradoxical at first sight, it is worth pondering the first question for a moment. A recent example may serve as illustration.

On September 22, 2020, Ben Bradshaw, a Labour MP in the British House of Commons, asked the following during Prime Minister's Questions:

> Does he think that the reason Germany and Italy have far lower COVID rates than us, with life continuing more or less normally, might be that they have locally and publicly run test and trace services that actually work?[1]

Prime Minister Boris Johnson replied:

> No, I don't, and I think the continual attacks on local test and trace and what NHS Test and Trace has done are undermining and unnecessary. Actually, there is an important difference between our country and many other countries around the world: our country is a freedom-loving country. If we look at the history of this country over the past 300 years, virtually every advance, from free speech to democracy, has come from this country. It is very difficult to ask the British population uniformly to obey guidelines in the way that is necessary.[2]

Within two days, these comments had elicited a response from the Italian President Sergio Mattarella, who said: "We Italians also love freedom, but we also care about seriousness,"[3] to which the Italian Minister for Health, Pierpaolo Sileri, added that "freedom comes from respecting rules."[4]

One might be tempted to dismiss this episode as a mere political spat in the heated and factious post-Brexit climate. But that would overlook the fact that different concepts of freedom (or "liberty" if one uses these two terms synonymously)[5] lie at the heart of the disagreement. While Prime Minister Johnson understands "freedom" to mean the absence of external constraints, so that every restriction or directive—including and especially the imposition of rules by the state—is tantamount to a loss of liberty, the statements by President Mattarella and Minister Sileri are underpinned by a notion of freedom that is not merely compatible with (certain) restrictions and state-imposed directives, but where rule-following can actually lead to an enhancement of liberty. The question then is: what accounts for this discrepancy?

We can find a clue to the explanation in a further example. On July 19, 2021, all COVID restrictions remaining in England at the time were lifted,[6] with the British government declaring "Freedom Day." For many citizens, formally speaking for all citizens, this was indeed a liberty-enhancing event, in the sense that they no longer needed to wear face coverings, but would thenceforth only do so voluntarily (and in practice to an ever-declining extent) on the basis of their own "common sense." Many others, however, did not perceive the lifting of restrictions as "liberating," but rather as a threat—particularly those members of society who had been unable take up the offer of a vaccination (for example on health- or age-related grounds), although they may have wanted to. For them, "Freedom Day" actually entailed a loss of liberty, because in order to minimize the risk of becoming infected, they would have to reduce their everyday social interaction. The "freedom" experienced by this part of the population—or, more precisely, the freedom of all citizens on this understanding of "freedom"—would only be reinstated or once again enlarged, all other things remaining equal, by re-imposing certain restrictions and state-imposed directives (such as mandatory face coverings). The example illustrates how strongly our understanding of "freedom" is colored by the perspective we adopt.

It is often said—in very rough-and-ready terms and (only) half in jest—that in England everything is allowed that is not expressly forbidden, while in continental Europe everything is prohibited unless it has been expressly authorized by the state. That is of course a gross and, as will be seen, misleading exaggeration; yet it demonstrates nicely quite how central the idea of an unrestricted room for maneuver is to the core notion of "freedom" in Britain (and, since it is even more pronounced in the United States, to the Anglo-American notion more generally). It is this concept of freedom which underlies Prime Minister Johnson's statement in the House of Commons and which also bestowed the "Freedom Day" on England. By contrast, when the Italian politicians stress that freedom and rule-following are ultimately compatible, they are placing the exercise and enjoyment of individual freedom into a broader societal context and recognize that this context may give birth to a new, different form of individual freedom.

"POSITIVE" AND "NEGATIVE" LIBERTY

The famous philosopher Isaiah Berlin once put his finger on the two very different understandings of "freedom" or "liberty."[7] On the one hand, there is the classical "negative" concept of liberty, which defines liberty from the perspective of the individual as the absence of external constraints. The more room for maneuver the individual has to do as he/she[8] likes, the greater their freedom or liberty in this (negative) sense. This can be contrasted with—or rather to this can be added—a "positive" conception of liberty, which focuses not on the *freedom from* something, but on the *freedom to* do or be something, in particular the liberty to lead a self-determined life. Enjoying liberty in this sense basically means being one's own master. This does not necessarily indicate or entail the absence of restrictions; what it does mean is that any restrictions are self-imposed. The matter becomes clear when one considers the following example: a person who makes use of their freedom of contract (an emanation of their "private autonomy") and enters into a binding legal agreement is thereby giving up a part of their negative freedom in order to achieve—through the law—a particular self-defined goal.

Isaiah Berlin did not invent the distinction between "positive" and "negative" liberty, but he was harking back to a whole series of philosophical trends and ideas. Only a few of these can be considered here against the backdrop of the theme to which the current Convoco Edition is dedicated, with special regard to the individual and social dimensions of freedom/liberty. While the latter distinction is by no means congruous with that between "negative" and "positive" liberty, there is nevertheless a close relationship and indeed interaction between the two.

IS FREEDOM OR LIBERTY EVEN CONCEIVABLE WITHOUT SOCIETY?

The different aspects of freedom and liberty (individual freedom and liberties depending for their realization on the existence of a broader social context) may easily mislead us into overlooking a fundamental preliminary question, namely whether freedom is something that is even conceivable without some sort of society.

Envisage a person living like Robinson Crusoe alone on a remote island. This person is not subject to any constraints other than those imposed by nature. It is nonetheless not intuitively obvious to describe them as being "free" or enjoying "liberty." They are no more "free" than the animals surrounding them, and (since humans are confined to moving about on the earth's surface) in many respects less "free" than the birds in the sky. One might therefore conclude that "freedom," even "negative freedom," becomes a rather shallow notion if removed from its societal embeddedness. And it is altogether impossible to give legal significance to the concept of freedom or liberty without relying on the normative ties that bind society together. The normative context is what elevates our ideal of "freedom" beyond the purely descriptive level. If, therefore, we are considering the individual and the social dimensions of freedom or liberty in what follows, it is important to recognize that we are concerned with notions that exist *within* a societal legal framework—specifically within the modern state—which are either directed primarily at fending off intrusions into a person's negative freedom or whose first and foremost concern is to secure the liberty of participating in particular social processes. In English, the distinction between these two different orientations is sometimes reflected in a nuanced contrast between "freedom" and "liberty," although the terms are more often used synonymously.[9]

SAFETY AS AN INDISPENSABLE PRECONDITION OF FREEDOM

There is another reason why the social context of freedom matters. Before people can go about enjoying or exercising their freedom(s), either individually or as part of a group, it is an indispensable precondition that they should be protected from the danger of others encroaching upon their life and threatening their physical integrity. A guaranteed basic level of security is a precondition of all significant freedom; and to provide this minimum level of safety is, in today's world, the role of the state.

This insight was formulated with particular force and clarity by Thomas Hobbes during the 17th century, in his reflections on the social contract. In what is probably his most famous work, *Leviathan*, Hobbes explains that it is only possible to overcome the "war of every man against every man" which pertains in the "state of nature" by the existence or institution of a powerful sovereign.[10] Under the social contract envisaged by Hobbes, people give up a part of their "natural liberty" and transfer to the sovereign in particular their innate right of self-defense. This sovereign, in turn, has to be strong enough to provide the security they need in order to live free from existential threats.[11]

The COVID-19 crisis has thrown us all brutally back onto Hobbes' security *leitmotif*. Of course that particular danger is a natural one, emanating from a virus rather than from man-made disasters such as civil war, crime, or terrorism. Yet few of us, if anyone, could have imagined at the start of 2020 that Europe would soon experience strict lockdowns with curfews being imposed, large parts of the economy brought to a near-standstill, and schools remaining closed for months on end. One may debate whether the tough measures were ultimately too high a price to pay for the breathing space they bought us (maintaining a by-and-large functioning health system and saving a great number of lives, although the actual number is hard to quantify with any degree of precision). What seems indisputable, however, is that the restrictions on freedom we experienced were imposed specifically with a view to protecting citizens' lives and that on the whole the population accepted them as such.

DEFENSIVE FUNDAMENTAL RIGHTS PROTECTING NEGATIVE FREEDOM

Although meaningful freedom therefore presupposes a sufficient level of personal safety on the one hand, the "negative" freedom of the individual must, on the other hand, be protected from unnecessary or disproportionate encroachments on the part of the state.[12] This requires there to be a robust set of defensive fundamental rights, which are often elevated to hold a special constitutional status. Germany's Basic Law, for instance, enumerates these rights very prominently in a catalogue deliberately located at its very beginning; and within the jurisprudence of the German Federal Constitutional Court,[13] the so-called "general freedom of action" (rooted in Article 2(1) of the Basic Law) has emerged as a "default fundamental right" protecting individuals against incursions into their freedom whenever the matter is not already covered by a more specific provision (such as freedom of expression in Article 5, freedom of association in Article 9, etc.). In practice, this means that *every* restriction on freedom and liberty imposed by the state requires a compelling legal justification.

In light of this fundamental rights position, it will be clear that the above-mentioned, oft-cited statement comparing the degree of freedom available to individuals in England and on the Continent (i.e. whether a system starts from a default position of freedom or of state authorization) actually distorts the real contrast. For if one looks closely at the issue one finds that "negative freedom" nowadays actually enjoys greater legal protection in many countries than in the self-declared motherland of freedom. As the United Kingdom does not have a written constitution, citizens' "defensive" fundamental rights are merely enshrined in what is technically simple primary legislation—and even that only since the enactment of the Human Rights Act 1998. The traditional doctrine of "Parliamentary Sovereignty" or "Supremacy" theoretically enables the UK legislator to effect or to authorize by a simple majority what may be the most severe infringements of basic liberties, without any possibility for a domestic court to intervene and stop the violation.

One reason why it long seemed (and in the eyes of some still seems) unnecessary to define and set in stone clear defensive rights against the state, or at any rate vis-à-vis the legislator, is that England and the UK generally regards itself not merely as the motherland of freedom, but also as a motherland of democracy. In its long history it never needed to extricate itself by force from a foreign power (as the United States had to), nor did it experience in the early modern era an extreme form of absolutism with an ensuing bloody and violent revolution (as happened in France),[14] and it was also spared the terrible dictatorships which blighted so much of the 20th century and completely subverted the rule of law (as in Germany during the Nazi era). By and large, the UK's unwritten constitution and its institutions functioned well and prevented excesses. This is why it is not surprising that "negative freedom" is still seen as the intuitive and self-evident basis of all social life within the state, rather than as something requiring special legal protection in express terms.

PARTICIPATION RIGHTS PROTECTING POSITIVE FREEDOM

It is mainly the continental tradition which emphasizes that there exists, beside the "negative" aspect of freedom, also a "positive" side, and furthermore, that a self-determined reduction in the scope of the former can under certain circumstances lead to an increase in the latter.

On the premise that it is impossible for an individual to be completely and absolutely "free" within a given society (if only because different people's respective spheres of action have to be delineated), we can see that the individual will inevitably be subject to some restrictions. The question then is how the process by which such restrictions are imposed can be made as compatible with freedom as it can possibly be. The French philosopher Jean-Jacques Rousseau formulated the challenge as follows:

> The problem is to find a form of association which will defend and protect with the whole common force the person and goods of each associate, and in which each, while uniting himself with all, may still obey himself alone, and remain as free as before.[15]

Recognizing that restrictions on a person's negative freedom are least invasive to freedom as a whole if they are (or can count as being) self-imposed is enormously important and has huge repercussions. Rousseau identifies the social contract as the solution to this conundrum. His social contract is very different from the similarly named construct proposed by Hobbes. While on Hobbes' account individuals forgo the absolute "freedom" they have in the state of nature in order to achieve a minimum level of security in the war of every man against every man, Rousseau maintains that although the contracting parties give up a part of their "natural liberty" under the social contract, at the same time they acquire a new form of freedom, namely "civil liberty." He achieves this by imputing to individuals the "general will" or *volonté générale*—a will formed by society as a whole—so as to make it their *own* will. In this way, any restrictions on individual citizens' (negative) freedom can count as being self-imposed and thus as emanations of every citizen's (positive) liberty.

A liberal democracy, of course, requires the imputation of the general will to be something that happens not counterfactually and fictitiously, but to be based on the involvement of citizens in the democratic process. This is why the individual's liberty within the state needs to be shored up by meaningful opportunities for democratic participation in the processes that shape public opinion and determine political decision-making. Gold standard here is the right to participate on an equal footing with others in free and secret general elections. It is buttressed by a series of defensive fundamental rights all of which are particularly relevant to forming public opinion and thus the general will, such as for example the right to freely hold and voice an opinion or the freedom of the press.

COEXISTENCE OF (AND BALANCE BETWEEN) POSITIVE AND NEGATIVE FREEDOM

Even though positive and negative freedom often interact in the way just outlined, it is clear that the existence of one type of freedom or liberty does not necessarily guarantee the existence of the other. Some authoritarian states are known for leaving substantial scope for individual freedom of action and thereby foster negative liberty, without at the same time promoting the positive liberty that allows individuals to participate meaningfully in the democratic process. Equally conceivable, in theory at least, is a democratic form of government which respects participatory rights and thus facilitates positive freedom, while at the same time allowing detailed rules to be imposed on the everyday life of its citizens and restricting, in particular, the (negative) freedom of minorities quite radically.

Ideally, however, a society will combine negative freedom and positive liberty in such a way as to achieve a balance between both. Guaranteeing citizens' rights to participate in the political process is key in ensuring that restrictions on their negative freedoms can count as self-imposed and that they are moreover referable to an exercise in positive liberty. (That said, it is of course true that not all members of society will in fact be actively eligible to vote or passively electable, but usually only those above a certain age who are nationals of the state in question.) At the same time, every human being needs to be guaranteed a non-violable sphere of core negative freedom and liberty which cannot be undermined or circumvented by others exercising their positive liberty in the political arena. This forestalls the danger of a minority falling victim to a dictatorship by the majority. All in all, therefore, the degree of freedom and liberty that a society has to offer is determined by two different factors, namely on the one hand the measure of personal maneuvering space accorded to individuals (to do or not to do as they like), and on the other hand, how reliably and well the democratic process functions.

RELATIONSHIP BETWEEN FREEDOM AND EQUALITY

It is nowadays quite common to portray "equality" as the great antagonist to freedom, and to perceive the relationship between these postulates as being full of tension. Underlying this view is the assumption that societies tend to become less equal the more freedom they allow, and that—conversely—a greater degree of equality can only be achieved at the price of imposing greater restrictions on people's personal freedom. Yet interestingly, freedom and equality were not always regarded as antagonists or being essentially incompatible. When these concepts first rose to prominence in early modern times in the wake of the Age of Enlightenment, they were actually thought of as being mutually complimentary. Freedom and equality presupposed each other and were seen as twin values intended to be realized together. This is particularly noticeable in the motto of the French Revolution, which placed freedom or liberty (*liberté*) right next to equality (*égalité*) and listed both even before the value of solidarity or fraternity (*fraternité*). The complementarity is also visible in the way the social contract is constructed. For example, according to Rousseau, the contract by which liberty within society becomes possible is concluded between parties who are (at least formally) equals. It is what accounts for the binding nature of the covenant and what then leads to a society of free and equal citizens.

It was not until sometime in the 19th century that perceptions changed and attention started to shift to a more "substantive" rather than a purely formal conception of equality. It became clear that the unbridled exercise of freedom by one part of society (the strong members) could contribute to the weakening of another part (the disadvantaged members) and that existing inequalities might thereby be perpetuated and exacerbated. Freedom and equality thus increasingly came to be understood as values needing to be weighed up against one another and to be brought into some sort of a balance. In modern constitutions such as Germany's Basic Law, freedom and equality are still enshrined side by side, but in the knowledge that what is commonly referred to as "practical concordance" [*praktische Konkordanz*] between them has to be achieved. The notion of "social justice"—and its exact meaning—is what has since taken center stage in the political debate about such balancing acts.

As far as the private relations between individuals are concerned, the starting point of deliberations is usually the ideal of liberty. We typically ask how far individual liberty has to be restrained in order to satisfy the equality postulate. Equality has, after all, been described as the "liberty of weaker parties."[16] To give just one example of this process occurring in practice: during the 20th century, first courts and then legislators all over Europe began to scrutinize the "fairness" and "reasonableness" of pre-formulated standard terms (especially) in consumer contracts, and subsequently they even inserted into general contract law certain anti-discrimination provisions; all this instead of simply leaving the content of transactions entirely up to the balance of power between the contracting parties. The aim of these judicial and legislative interventions was to strengthen and, where necessary, to protect structurally disadvantaged parties when contracting.

In more recent times, parts of the literature have sought to invert the basic position, starting from a general principle of equal treatment applicable not merely in the public sphere, but reaching all the way into the realm of people's private lives. Derogations from the stipulated general principle of equal treatment, so the argument runs, ought only to be permissible if and to the extent that the protection of individual liberty or similarly important values require it.[17] The danger with this account is that it may suggest (albeit inadvertently and without it being intended) that the exercise of freedom and liberty *always* requires some sort of justification. Yet if that were the case, freedom would no longer be a value *per se* deserving of protection in and of itself; instead, freedom and liberty would become instrumental values aimed as furthering certain social goals. On such an instrumental conception, however, "freedom" suddenly begins to look extremely fragile and vulnerable.

It is arguably easiest to reconcile the postulates of freedom and equality not by seeking to erase all inequalities with respect to the distribution of material goods, but by ensuring that there is a level playing field and thus understanding equality to mean an "equality of opportunities." This enables all members of society to avail themselves of equal freedom, but is at the same time compatible with an uneven distribution of material goods.

RIGHTS TO CLAIM CERTAIN BENEFITS AND DUTIES OF PARTICIPATION

This leads us to the question of *how* it is possible to ensure genuine equality of opportunities for individuals and an equal ability actively to use their freedoms. It has already been noted above that our conception of what "freedom" is and how it is best ring-fenced as a matter of law has changed or—more precisely—has become broader. Defensive rights protecting negative freedom are buttressed and supplemented by participation rights allowing individuals to actively shape their lives. However, neither the negative freedom from restrictions nor the positive liberty to participate in societal processes are of real benefit so long as the individual concerned is unable, on account of poverty or for other reasons, to make use of these rights and thus to realize their (negative or positive) liberty. By way of example, if someone is homeless, then the fact that the state safeguards the strict privacy of a person's private home and declares their residence to be "inviolable" will not be of much use to them. And a person who cannot read or write will in practice experience a much reduced "freedom of contract" and will be unable to participate fully in the processes that shape public opinion and channel it into a democratic form of government.

It is for this reason that the modern welfare state provides, besides the traditional defensive and participatory rights, certain rights and benefit entitlements consisting, in particular, of guaranteed minimum social standards (such as a basic subsistence level) and the provision of a core public infrastructure (including, for instance, the fundamental right to be educated in a school, as expressly recognized in a recent judgment of Germany's Federal Constitutional Court).[18] Of course every society will ultimately have to decide for itself how much to invest in such liberty-enhancing social measures.

The situation becomes much trickier where state support results in active interventionism or even paternalism, for it then looks as if the state's well-meaning "support" scheme aimed at enhancing liberty might in reality amount to an infringement of the individual's freedom. Here a careful case-by-case scrutiny is called for. While it may not be hard to justify imposing a duty on all children to attend school, coercive measures vis-à-vis adults (such as requiring a homeless person to live in a state-allocated residential unit) are all but impossible to defend. After all, how can we force someone to be "free" and to accept certain benefits in order to live their lives in accordance with the freedom ideals of others? To attempt to do so would achieve the polar opposite of positive liberty as it would prevent people from being their own masters.

A related question, which may be added here before concluding, is whether it is possible to conceive not only of individual *rights* to participate in society, but personal or citizenship *duties* to do so. It is generally accepted that there is a *moral* correlation between individual freedom and individual responsibility. Whether there is also (or can be) a *legal* correlation depends on the type of freedom under consideration. If one thinks of negative freedom, i.e. a room for maneuver ring-fenced by a set of defensive rights, then the answer is clear: the use of this type of freedom is, by definition, entirely at the discretion of the individual. Responsible conduct requires no more than that the individual's actions do not cause harm to others—and this postulate will already be factored into the way the law delineates the individual's maneuvering space in the first place.

As regards positive liberty oriented towards participation in society, the problem of responsibility lies not so much in getting involved, but in people forgoing their opportunities to do so. One could therefore ask whether the existence of certain participation rights (such as the right to vote) should be flanked by legally enforceable duties to make use of these rights (as, for instance, in the case of compulsory voting in Australia). There is an evident counter-argument which one may be able to overcome, but which cannot be dismissed outright: imposing a duty to exercise a positive liberty amounts to a clear restriction of negative freedom. In other words, genuine freedom requires individuals to be free *not* to exercise their liberties.

EPILOGUE

After a relatively relaxed summer during which the COVID-19 pandemic appeared to subside partly on account of the newly developed vaccines, the onslaught of a fourth wave of infections in the autumn of 2021 led to a heated debate about the pros and cons of making vaccination compulsory. Austria was the first Member State of the European Union to enact legislation to this effect. This is another context in which the question "How much freedom must we forgo to be free?" becomes hugely topical. In a jointly authored article published in the *Frankfurter Allgemeine Zeitung* in November 2021, the Minister-Presidents of the German states of Baden-Württemberg and Bavaria, Winfried Kretschmann and Markus Söder, made the case for compulsory vaccinations by arguing as follows: "A duty to be vaccinated does not amount to an infringement of fundamental liberties. Rather, it is the precondition for us all regaining our liberty."[19] This once again emphasizes the various different—individual as well as societal—dimensions of freedom and liberty.

POSTSCRIPT

It seems appropriate to close with a postscript taking the themes addressed in this chapter yet further forward. After the German text of this chapter was finalized, the Omicron-variant of COVID-19 caused a surge of infections all over Europe between December 2021 and February 2022. The United Kingdom and England in particular, still led by Boris Johnson's Tory government, imposed fewer restrictions than most other countries and, death rates nonetheless remaining relatively low, apparently got away with it. This led some to question whether perhaps the scientific projections which had warned of the potentially devastating effects of Omicron were misguided from the start, and calls soon increased to jettison all remaining COVID restrictions (which had been re-imposed in late fall) as soon as possible—"Freedom Day 2.0", so to speak. Prime Minister Johnson, at this point beleaguered by a flood of "Partygate" revelations indicating serial rule-breaking on a massive scale in 10 Downing Street, appeared only too happy to oblige in order to divert attention from his government's failings. To this, the *Guardian* columnist Will Hutton responded by reminding readers that the Omicron wave was in fact attenuated by the public itself who, partly spurred by the alarming projections, had on the whole exercised great restraint in social interaction over Christmas and had voluntarily refrained from mingling:

> It was our new behavior, as much as state rules, which drove the better-than-expected outcome. We were, in philosopher Isaiah Berlin's famous formulation, practitioners of positive liberty—taking control of our individual destinies through acting together. By contrast, Tory libertarians are really Big Brother imposers of Berlin's negative liberty, defining liberty not in terms of individuals trying to control their life in concert with others but wholly in terms of removing what they describe as coercive state restrictions and obstacles.[20]

This takes us right back to the theme addressed in the introductory paragraphs. What may look paradoxical at first sight—how one can gain freedom by forgoing it—becomes perfectly intelligible once we recognize that "freedom" has a number of different dimensions and that "positive" liberty within a society can indeed be enhanced if individuals collectively sacrifice a small part of their "negative" freedom.

Notes

1. Hansard, House of Commons Debate, (September 22, 2020), vol. 680, col. 814 (emphasis added).
2. Ibid.
3. Reuters, news item of September 24, 2020, https://www.reuters.com/article/health-coronavirus-italy-britain-idINKCN26F27U (accessed December 6, 2021).
4. Angela Giuffrida, "Italian president rebuts Johnson's 'freedom' remarks over restrictions" in *The Guardian*, September 24, 2020, https://www.theguardian.com/world/2020/sep/24/italian-president-rebuts-johnsons-freedom-remarks-over-covid-19-restrictions (accessed December 6, 2021).
5. See note 9 below and the text thereto.
6. As a result of the devolution settlements reached in the late 1990s, Scotland, Wales, and Northern Ireland each have the right to enact their own rules concerning public health measures, and they have done so in different ways.
7. Isaiah Berlin, "Two Concepts of Liberty", Inaugural Lecture of October 31, 1958, published in *Four Essays on Liberty* (Oxford: Oxford University Press, 1969), pp. 118–172.
8. In the following, the gender-neutral plural form "their/them" will be used to denote "he/him" or "she/her."

9. While such subtle nuances may be ascribed to the words "freedom" and liberty" in the English usage, they are actually not replicated in other languages with which the words are etymologically connected. German uses the same term [*Freiheit*] across the board, and the same is also true of French [*liberté*].

10. Thomas Hobbes, *Leviathan: Or the Matter, Forme and Power of a Commonwealth, Ecclesiasticall and Civil* (first published London: Andrew Crooke, 1651).

11. Note, however, that the social contract according to Hobbes is technically not concluded between the individual and the state, but only among the subjects themselves ("covenant of every man with every man").

12. In legal discourse, one often finds the "negative" aspect of freedom reduced to the proposition that an individual can refrain from exercising a liberty (such as, for example, by *not* expressing an opinion or *not* practicing a religion). Here, however, the focus is on whether there exists in principle a protected sphere within which individuals are free to do as they like—be it by actively using their liberty (in the "positive" sense) or by refraining from doing so. Freedom is in both cases secured by a protecting "negative" shield against external interference. In this regard, the present notion of "negative freedom" may be somewhat broader than the one outlined above; it is primarily concerned with the defensive function of protecting fundamental rights.

13. The foundational case is the decision of the German Federal Constitutional Court of June 6, 1989, BVerfGE 80, 137, known as "Reiten im Walde" [Riding in the woods].

14. It is true that the English Civil War (1642–51), the Restoration period, and the ensuing Glorious Revolution eventually resulted in the enactment of the Bill of Rights 1689. However, this piece of legislation was primarily aimed at strengthening Parliament vis-à-vis the Monarch and

did rather less to bestow individual defensive rights upon citizens seeking to fend off interferences by the state as such.

15. Jean-Jacques Rousseau, *Du contrat social: ou Principes du droit politique* (first published Amsterdam: Marc Michel Rey, 1762), ch. 6, here cited after the classic English translation by G.D.H. Cole.

16. Expression coined by Walter Leisner, *Der Gleichheitsstaat: Macht durch Nivellierung* (Berlin: Duncker & Humblot, 1980), p. 34.

17. See especially Michael Grünberger, *Personale Gleichheit: Der Grundsatz der Gleichbehandlung im Zivilrecht* (Baden-Baden: Nomos, 2013).

18. Decision of the German Federal Constitutional Court of November 19, 2921 known as "Bundesnotbremse II: Schulschließungen" [Federal pandemic emergency brake II; school closures], which acknowledged this right as being of fundamental constitutional significance.

19. Winfried Kretschmann and Markus Söder, "Die Impfpflicht schützt die Freiheit" in *Frankfurter Allgemeine Zeitung*, November 22, 2021, https://www.faz.net/aktuell/politik/inland/corona-impfpflicht-von-soeder-und-winfried-kretschmann-gefordert-17647078.html (accessed December 6, 2021).

20. Will Hutton, "Like most, I relish life opening up. But this libertarian dash for the Covid exit is reckless" in *The Guardian*, March 13, 2022, https://www.theguardian.com/commentisfree/2022/feb/13/dash-for-covid-exit-proves-political-virus-lbertarianism-rampant (accessed February 14, 2022).

CHAPTER 10

HOW MUCH FREEDOM MUST WE FORGO TO BE FREE? SECURITY AND FREEDOM ARE INTERDEPENDENT

BRUNO KAHL

During the French Revolution, soldiers from Marseille entered Paris singing a song written in 1792, which went on to become the French national anthem. The sixth stanza of the world-famous *Marseillaise* reads:

Liberty, cherished Liberty
Join the struggle with your defenders!

What these verses tell us is that freedom is not God-given and unconditional; rather it needs defenders to stand up for it. Which brings us to our topic: how much freedom must we forgo to be free? This question is paradoxical only at first sight, as it indeed characterizes the freedom of every individual, in that it can never exist absolutely, and that it can only ever be experienced and lived in relative terms.

If we ask ourselves what freedom actually is, the answer pertaining to our coexistence in German society is provided by the Basic Law. Germany's Constitution was created under particular historical circumstances and out of a certain kind of political awareness. In light of the oppression, persecution, and extermination that took place between 1933 and 1945, rights to freedom were afforded particularly high priority in the Constitution of Germany's Second Republic for very good reason: they were intended to protect the individual and their rights in the future against arbitrary state decisions and violations, such as were imposed during the twelve years of the Third Reich. If hitherto the value of freedom in German society has often been given disproportionately greater weight than, for example, the value of security, this is rooted in 20th-century German history, in its failures and catastrophes. Freedom and security, however, are by no means opposites that can be played off against one another—they are mutually dependent. In this essay I would like to examine this more closely.

Unlimited freedom means merely arbitrariness and anarchy—but if it is any way enshrined in law, it is the law of "might is right". Anyone dreaming of the ideal of unlimited, absolute freedom will certainly not find it in a failed state in which every kind of freedom has been suffocated by violence and chaos. My academic teacher Josef Isensee believed that the connection between freedom and security was so evident that he afforded security the status of a fundamental right as well. And he quoted a journalist reporting from a country involved in a civil war: "It is a fundamental human right not to be shot in the street. That fundamental right was [...] no longer guaranteed. Only when it is guaranteed again can we discuss other fundamental rights."[1] From this we can conclude that every individual freedom is based on order within the state. Without security there is no peace, without peace there is no freedom. War is the complete negation of freedom, and we know that civil war is the worst, the cruelest, the most unrestrained kind of war. If people want to live together in peace, unlimited individual freedom cannot exist. The freedom of one individual only extends to the point that delimits the freedom of another individual. However, in a democratic constitutional state, absolute security is equally impossible to achieve: any attempt to establish one hundred percent security leads in the medium term to dictatorship and terror, which are also the complete opposite of freedom. As is so often the case in human life, this too is about doing all things in moderation to create the best possible balance between freedom and security in and for our society.

Thirty years ago, the end of the Cold War, German unity, and the unification of Europe offered us the short-lived illusion that all global political tensions would now be resolved and that we were facing the end of history and everlasting peace. Nothing seemed to stand in the way of the flourishing of freedom and freedom alone. By 9/11 at the latest, whose 20th anniversary took place in 2021, we had been rudely awakened from this fantasy. Debate about the balance between security and freedom was given new relevance by these dramatic events. We remember the heated discussions and hard-line talk of that time. Since the terror attacks of September 11, 2001, the world has not become more peaceful—on the contrary. We now live in a thoroughly globalized and digitalized world that is moving ever closer towards us, becoming more and more confusing, and also increasingly insecure. Reliable sources and information are all the more important in order to understand this world and navigate our way. This also applies to politics in particular: whether in Germany, Austria, or Great Britain governments need facts and assessments they can rely on in their foreign and security policy decision-making. In Germany it is our job, the task of the Federal Intelligence Service (BND), to generate security in this way.

And that brings me to the threats to freedom that Germany is facing, because the threats from international terrorism, for example, have by no means been averted. Rather, various Islamist extremists and jihadists who take their orders from the "Islamic State" (IS) in Germany and Europe continue to endanger the peace and freedom in which we live. The IS territorial project may have failed because it has no "state" in Syria or Iraq, but we can see that IS is reverting to "classic" terrorist activities both underground and through networks. Their focus includes Europe and Germany. Moreover, we can see that the rift between Shiites and Sunnis is widening and creating the potential for ever new conflicts. In this context, the bad news is that the lines between terrorism and traditional criminal activity are becoming blurred. In many regions, clans, militias, and terrorist groups are currently benefiting from this; they are violent, unscrupulous, and increasingly successful in pursuit of their agenda. It is a disaster for the local population that there is no alternative to this as long as there are no strong, recognized state structures. In many cases, the hopes for rapid improvement are unfortunately illusory. This applies to regions in the Near and Middle East as well as to parts of North Africa and sub-Saharan Africa, and the sphere of influence of these groups has recently extended to include countries further south. Here, too, the well-known connection between protection and obedience, between freedom and security can be seen once more—a lesson that Europe learned through bloody wars of religion, and that other regions of the world now have to learn just as arduously and with heavy losses. And terror entails loss of freedom not only where it is perpetrated but also in Europe: remote-controlled attacks, migration, and imported criminality always mean a challenge to and restriction of freedom in Europe—even if it is just the freedom of generations to come, which according to the German Federal Constitutional Court can be calculated down to the last decimal point.[2]

So how free are people when, in the heart of Europe, they have to live with the possibility of a bomb exploding in the subway on their way to work, a bomb planted by an Islamist terrorist? Or that they might be run over by a truck at a Christmas market or on a seaside promenade?

In addition, new dangers are being created by the rapid advance of digitalization and globalization: we are experiencing hybrid threats that, for example, hit the German Bundestag as early as 2015 in the form of cyber-attacks. And expert hackers are operating today on behalf of the state even in Iran and North Korea. How free is the political party whose accounts are hacked and leaked—an activity that's particularly popular during election campaigns, for example in the US in 2016? How free is the democracy and human rights activist who is imitated using "deep-fakes" to appear in video conferences he never actually participated in—as happened repeatedly to Russian anti-corruption lawyer Alexei Navalny's chief-of-staff Leonid Volkov?[3] How free is the patient in a hospital whose infrastructure is hacked, whose IT is blocked, or whose electricity is cut off by criminals who are blackmailing the hospital using ransomware, as has happened several times in recent years in the German state of North Rhine-Westphalia, for example?

Another challenge shared by all intelligence services is the increasing attractiveness of authoritarian/populist politics both at home and abroad. Major ideological shifts are underway: we are seeing attempts by authoritarian states to influence open societies and market economies in the West—and indeed using illegitimate means. Both pressure and manipulative incentives are being used. We are experiencing both direct influence and creeping indirect influence. Today the ideological battle is no longer between communism and capitalism, but between constitutional, value-based democracies on the one hand and emerging authoritarian models of society on the other. The latter appear attractive, as they are ostensibly stable, militarily strong, and often also economically very successful, especially since decisions, be they political or economic in nature (for example decisions about large infrastructure projects such as airports, freeways, or railroads) are made ruthlessly and implemented quickly without any supposedly annoying procedures or lengthy debates to hold them up. In these models, social freedoms are regarded with disdain and replaced by other priorities, namely economic prosperity, nationalism, or religion. Such models differentiate their own society positively by comparison with the West, which is discriminated against as "unstable" (financial crisis), "swamped by foreigners" (migration), "decadent" (no innate binding values), and "disintegrating" (Brexit). The target group of these narratives is primarily their own population, but they also have an impact on Europe—and penetrate deep into our society.

Authoritarian, repressive systems, led by a strong central power, and which are economically relatively successful, are thus becoming a popular alternative model to Western liberal systems—popular even in the most elevated circles of Western society. Since the legendary films of Beatles concerts in the 1960s, we have not seen such devoted fandom than that shown by the German captains of industry when they took part in a government delegation to visit the Chinese President, Xi Jinping. China's construction of the world's largest airport in Beijing in a very short space of time is indeed impressive. Not so long ago, however, the same country told a German premium manufacturer that it had better not use the Dalai Lama in its advertising if it wanted to carry on selling cars in China. As a result, the company apologized and cancelled the adverts. Similarly, at the request of the Chinese government, the science publisher Springer Nature censored its own Internet service in China, deleting topics such as Tibet and Taiwan. How free are German companies, then, if they are dependent on China? How free is Germany if it can no longer criticize China for human rights violations because it is afraid of losing sales and jobs in the automotive industry?

In this growing systemic conflict between constitutional, value-based democracies on the one hand

and modern, increasingly dictatorship-like autocracies on the other, we Germans and Europeans must face up to the uncomfortable question of how we want to behave in the long term, and if we want or can develop a strategy to do this, and what such a strategy would be. For example, we have to ask ourselves self-critically whether international cooperation should even be encouraged—and only for its own sake—if individual states only use the undoubted advantages of multilateralism to pursue their own aggressive and autocratic policies at the expense of our free, democratic societies. We have to ask ourselves whether we want to tolerate individual state actors who accept multilateral structures only ostensibly, in order to undermine our liberal world order from within. Postwar history shows us that, unfortunately, multilateral cooperation has not so far succeeded in convincing the enemies of the Western, open, liberal, and democratic constitutional state of the advantages of our social order. Rather, we must admit that these states have achieved their ascendancy even within the global democratic community.

I am well aware that one should take care when drawing historical parallels. Nevertheless, I would like to venture a comparison: the Weimar Republic collapsed because German's nascent democracy was unable to assert itself against its enemies. Between 1929 and 1933, the Weimar Constitution became a victim of its legalistic, positivistic interpreters. Through their naive trust in established law and a lack of awareness of the material content of the law, of the values on which the law is based, and which the Weimar Constitution therefore wanted to protect and uphold, they ultimately surrendered the Republic to its enemies even "in good conscience" through the Enabling Act. As the saying goes, a majority is a majority, even if it wants to abolish the principle of majority rule. This is a lesson that has been learned by the Basic Law, which protects its value against "legal" abolition. Enemies of the Constitution can no longer come to power—equally because our sister authority, the Federal Office for the Protection of the Constitution, are monitoring them.

But a similar danger and trap are threatening us today in the international arena. We have to be careful that, as overly uncritical multilateralists, we do not end up sacrificing the very multilateral world order that we actually want to protect and defend by abandoning it to its enemies. Today there are some powerful states in the world that support multilateralism only as long as it serves their aggressive interests. I am not calling for the recurring fashion for isolationism or "decoupling." But even more dangerous, because it conceals real interests, is a value-free, purely power-oriented multilateralism that only claims universal freedoms as long as they benefit from it, but gets rid of them as soon as it no longer needs them. For example, in May 2017, China succeeded in having its "One Belt, One Road Initiative" adopted as one of the United Nations' Sustainable Development Goals. But at the same time China disregards the rulings of the Permanent Court of Arbitration regarding China's claims to sovereignty in the South China Sea. And the 17 + 1 Summit is merely an ostensibly multilateral format, which in truth firstly divides the European Union and secondly serves to blackmail its Members. So how free are the states of the democratic West when they commit themselves to certain rules and their observance in supranational organizations, while other states sit at the table, but only adhere to these decisions as they see fit, otherwise pursuing their selfish, aggressive interests at the expense of the global community?

In this tense multipolar situation, information is becoming increasingly important. To this end, Germany needs a strong foreign intelligence service more than ever. The Federal Intelligence Service works around the clock, seven days a week, to identify impending dangers for the Federal Republic of Germany in a timely fashion, to analyze new trouble spots, and to obtain and evaluate crucial information.

This responsible work requires concentration and prudence—but also general acceptance and social recognition. However, when it comes to taking precautions for the internal and external security of our country, skeptics and critics quickly resort to phrases like "surveillance state" or, in the context of the intelligence services, even "Stasi" and "Gestapo."[4] Amazingly, it is often these same critics of internal and external security measures who actively and uncompromisingly demand a particularly high level of security for the individual within society. State social benefits are just as readily accepted and demanded of the state as the same state is denied the right to take the steps necessary to ensure the security of its citizens. Instead, security policy is defamed as a restriction of individual freedom. This pronounced social statism is sometimes countered by massive state skepticism when it comes to the Federal Republic of Germany's security concerns. The security authorities experience this skepticism in political debates as well as in their day-to-day work. Here, the facts are turned completely on their head, and a distorted picture is painted in which the constitutionally legitimate security authorities, whose legal mandate is to protect the liberal social order, are portrayed as the real threat to freedom.

We in the intelligence services depend on society's consent if we are to do our work effectively and for the benefit of citizens, for despite all the necessary skepticism and sometimes justified criticism, we must not forget that the BND is one of the best-monitored intelligence services in the world. Alongside the Federal Chancellery, several parliamentary and other independent bodies as well as the Federal Audit Office, the Federal Administrative Court, and the Federal Commissioner for Data Protection and Freedom of Information are keeping a close eye on us. The Federal Republic's intelligence services also have a significant strategic advantage over the secret services in the above-mentioned autocracies that lack any parliamentary control. Public and open opinion-forming is the prerequisite for us as security authorities to receive a sustained mandate from society to shed light on imminent threats and fend them off. Only with such a mandate are we in a position to counteract these risks together and as a community. In autocracies, in which the secret services are used to shore up power against their own people, this is not possible and often completely undesired. We must make consistent use of this strength in our democracy because it fundamentally differentiates us from secret services that operate arbitrarily in other regions of the world as well as from criminal organizations in German history, which unfortunately are still too often thoughtlessly mentioned in the same breath as their constitutional successors.

The Federal Intelligence Service is a loyal and discreet service of the Federal Government. We need trust at home in order to be able to act confidentially abroad. Intelligence services are a necessary element of the rule of law. In France and Great Britain, this is a given, and even more so in the US and Israel. In Germany, many people only become aware of this when something goes wrong. In the inquiry into the attack on Berlin's Breitscheidplatz in 2016, the same people who previously wanted to deny the services legal and financial resources accused them completely unjustifiably of failure. European history, shaped for far too long by violence and war, gave us, with the help of the US after 1945 and again after 1989, the opportunity to develop a system based on freedom and peace. We have learned that freedom can only be realized if the state creates the necessary legal and factual conditions—and that means above all security for its citizens.

If we remain aware that the freedom that characterizes us as humans and that we have been gifted, as it were, has to be fought for time and again and also defended by the security authorities, it will no longer be so hard to find an intelligent and convincing answer to the question of how much freedom we *supposedly* must forgo in order to be *truly* free.

Notes

1. Josef Isensee, *Das Grundrecht auf Sicherheit. Zu den Schutzpflichten des freiheitlichen Verfassungsstaates* (Berlin/New York: De Gruyter, 1983), p. 19.
2. This refers to a decision by the German Federal Court in March 2021 that the German government had taken insufficient action on the reduction of greenhouse gas emissions, violating intertemporal guarantees of freedom. See Bundesverfassungsgericht, "Press Release no. 31/2021," https://www.bundesverfassungsgericht.de/SharedDocs/Pressemitteilungen/EN/2021/bvg21-031.html (accessed November 16, 2021).
3. See for example: Andrew Roth, "European MPs targeted by deep fake video calls imitating Russian opposition," April 22, 2021, https://www.theguardian.com/world/2021/apr/22/european-mps-targeted-by-deepfake-video-calls-imitating-russian-opposition (accessed November 16, 2021).
4. The Stasi [*Staatssicherheitsdienst*] was the State Security Service of the German Democratic Republic; the Gestapo [*Geheime Staatspolizei*] was the secret police of Nazi Germany.

CHAPTER 11

THE DANGERS OF THE NEW SUPERPOWER RIVALRY BETWEEN THE US AND CHINA

PETER WITTIG

I. FREEDOM ON THE DEFENSIVE?

Western-style democracies are apparently on the defensive. From a global perspective, it seems that liberal, constitution-based, democratic states are currently experiencing a downturn, while authoritarian states are increasing in number, for example Brazil, India, Mexico, Turkey, the Philippines, and Myanmar. Even within the European Union, individual states are not immune from the temptations of authoritarianism—think of Poland and Hungary. In the prestigious Freedom House Index, just 83 out of 210 countries and territories are rated "free."[1] *The Economist* magazine's Democracy Index identifies only 23 "full" democracies throughout the world.[2]

With the election of Donald Trump in 2016, the US must share some responsibility for this trend towards authoritarian states. The president of the leading Western power abdicated his role as standard bearer of the free democracies and sympathized with authoritarian regimes. On January 6, 2021, the world's oldest constitutional democracy ultimately faltered even on its foundations of freedom when the elected president contested his defeat, both encouraging and tolerating the storming of Congress, the symbol of American democracy. The new President, Joe Biden, promises a fundamental reset: a refocusing on proven alliances, diplomacy, and multilateral cooperation. However, he sees the aspiration to strengthen free, democratic states primarily in terms of offensive systemic competition with the camp of authoritarian states, above all China and Russia. A symbol of this reset, he said, was a "Summit for Democracy" announced at the beginning of Biden's term of office. It took place in December 2021. The question of who will be invited to such a democracy summit or who should be disregarded as "non-democratic" is naturally sensitive, in terms of political alliances as well. Freedom House considers as "free" and democratic only 77 of the 111 participating states. The other 34 states fall into the categories of "partly free" or "not free." The president has therefore opted for a "big tent" approach (instead of a core group of democracies), in order to make the systemic competition against the authoritarian states as broad as possible.

We are now more than ever in an era of renewed rivalry between the superpowers. The expectations or hopes of a convergence in systems after the end of the Cold War or, in the case of China, when it joined the World Trade Organization (WTO), have meanwhile been set aside. Today's rivalry between the US and China, however, differs from the earlier antagonism between the US and the Soviet Union, a military superpower that wanted to expand but lacked economic parity with the US. By contrast, the new superpower constellation of the US and China is a systemic rivalry between two politically very different but economically increasingly equal giants for the position of future global power.

II. ESCALATING TENSIONS

The relationship between the United States and China will undoubtedly be the most important strategic relationship over the next few decades. It is the central axis around which international politics and the global economy will revolve. The rivalry between these two superpowers is fiercer than ever. Should Europe, and especially Germany, be worried? Yes! The German "business model" works best in a world of multilateral cooperation and an open, rule-based trading system. Both are currently exposed to considerable dangers. However, there is no absolute historical necessity for the widespread gloomy prophecies of an inevitable clash between the two superpowers. The future is undecided. It is also conceivable that a scenario of increased cooperation between the two superpowers will develop in the future.

What are the drivers of conflict in this superpower rivalry?

- The struggle for economic and technological supremacy
- The competition between two fundamentally different ideological systems—if you will, a new type of ideological systemic competition:

Western democracies (under the albeit fragile leadership of the US) versus authoritarian states, in particular China
- The geopolitical conflict for global supremacy between an established superpower and a new, rising superpower. The ancient Greek historian Thucydides provided an early example of how such a conflict (between Sparta and Athens) can spin out of control. The immediate triggers of conflict are numerous: Taiwan (the most dangerous arena of conflict), Hong Kong, the South China Sea, the plight of the Uyghurs, cyberspace attacks, China's growing influence in Africa, South America, and also in parts of Europe, especially due to the gigantic infrastructure project of China's Belt and Road Initiative.

How do the two superpowers see each another—a decisive factor in the outbreak of conflicts? In geostrategic terms, the US sees China as the only enemy that can pose a threat. According to Washington, Russia is no longer in this league. The US is looking to the Pacific more than ever. Equally, the European allies have become less important, and in this President Biden is very much following in the tradition of his predecessor. "Tough on China": that is the consensus in Washington—almost the only subject that still unites Republicans and Democrats. China's economic rise—in part due to its practices contravening WTO regulations, according to the US—is to be slowed down, and China's dominance in Asia and its global reach are to be curbed. That is why the US is entering into new geostrategic alliances. On the one hand, there is the so-called Quad, a four-way alliance between the US, Japan, Australia, and India in the Indo-Pacific region; and on the other hand, AUKUS, a new triple alliance between the US, Australia, and the United Kingdom, which was signed in September 2021. The latter is intended to supply Australia with nuclear-powered submarines, but its strategic importance goes far beyond delivering boats. Both alliances are directed—more or less explicitly—against China's hegemonic aspirations in the Asian region. At the instigation of the US, NATO too has identified China as an exceptional new threat and adopted a position against China.

For its part, China considers the US to be in irreversible decline. For China, the toxic divisions in US society and the shameful withdrawal from Afghanistan are the latest visible signs of this. Beijing regards itself as on the historical path to the "great renaissance" of the Middle Kingdom. In fact, according to economic forecasts, China will catch up with the US as early as 2029. By its own admission, China wants to become the number one world power at the latest by 2049, the 100th anniversary of the founding of the People's Republic. China is preparing for this goal both strategically and in the long term: President Xi Jinping has embarked on the road of authoritarian leadership and the influence of the Communist Party has increased—with a new, intensive injection of ideology into politics, the goal of annexing Taiwan is stated in concrete terms, and the latest Five-Year Plan is imbued with the spirit of geopolitics, or rather geoeconomics, with aspirations to technological independence and global economic leadership.

III. THE SPIRAL OF CONFLICT CREATED BY ECONOMIC COERCIVE MEASURES

Is this a case of two unstoppable forces inevitably colliding? In the last few months, the spiral of conflict has at least carried on turning, especially in the imposition of coercive measures: tariffs, sanctions, export bans on strategic goods, investment restrictions, listing of undesirable companies, etc. A decisive milestone in the escalation of tension was the West's sanctions against China in spring 2021 in response to Beijing violating the human rights of the Uyghurs, the Muslim population living in Xinjiang Province. The US government branded the treatment of the Muslim minority as "genocide" and, along with the European Union, Canada, and the UK, imposed sanctions on Chinese officials. Beijing responded immediately and unusually harshly with counter-sanctions, targeting Western officials, critical lawmakers, and even research bodies. This was new, as until that point China's reaction to the US imposition of sanctions had been limited to verbal counterattacks. The new and clear message was that China will no longer put up with Western coercive measures and will react in a tit for tat manner.

IV. DECOUPLING OF NATIONAL ECONOMIES?

There has been much talk recently of "decoupling," the deliberate disentangling of ties between the American and Chinese economies. However, a more differentiated approach is on the agenda.

On the US side, we can see clear strategic trends towards isolating China in the high-tech sector. There are numerous examples: the extensive measures against Huawei, bans on the export of American high-tech to China, bans on investing in Chinese high-tech companies including Chinese chip manufacturers, pressure on foreign companies and governments to stop supplying Chinese chip manufacturers, etc. By contrast, the manufacturing sector has so far been less affected by US measures. On the capital markets and in the financial industry, however, isolation is almost non-existent—on the contrary. The flow of private US capital to China has increased significantly in recent years and Chinese capital is heavily invested in the US. However, the strong inflow of American capital into the Chinese high-tech and financial sectors has recently weakened after Beijing intervened massively to rein in its own large tech corporations. As a result, confidence on Wall Street has suffered.

But China too has shown tendencies towards decoupling. Let's take a look at their 14th Five-Year Plan for 2021–25, as it sheds light on China's future development. The Plan is permeated with the aspiration to make China independent of foreign powers. The key concept is the "dual circulation strategy," in which China must remain part of international circulation and global trade, defend its export markets, and strengthen the domestic export industry. At the same time, increasing emphasis is being placed on domestic circulation, by strengthening China's own industries and reducing dependency on external factors. Supply chains are to remain national or be relocated back into the country. The Five-Year Plan identifies seven strategic future industries that are central to economic development and national security and must therefore be developed autonomously, from artificial intelligence to the semiconductor industry, quantum computing to the exploitation of outer space. In addition, the standards-setting within the framework of "China Standards 2035" is one of Beijing's strategic focal points. China is increasingly defining its own norms and standards, which it then incorporates into international standards-setting, for example in the area of the Internet and the "Internet of Things", as well as in conventional industries where China is strong. Such a conflict with Western-style regulations and standards is already taking place in international standards-setting organizations, for example in the International Telecommunication Union.

In conclusion, on the US side, we cannot currently talk about widespread decoupling, but rather a partial decoupling that is limited to the tech sector. What we can see, however, is a clear tendency to split or separate the technology spheres from one another, be it through economic coercive measures or the divergence between regulation and standards-setting. In the long term, China's efforts to decouple from the US economy may even be more significant than the most recent US measures.

V. EUROPE AND THE SUPERPOWERS—BETWEEN A ROCK AND A HARD PLACE?

The growing Sino-American antagonism risks trapping Europe between a rock and a hard place—in the worst-case scenario, industry would have to choose between the American and the Chinese markets. How can the EU hold up against the competition between these two world powers? The European Union is not a major geopolitical superpower, but it is a "global trade power." It is fully capable of taking action on issues of foreign trade because all Member States have ceded their national competences to the EU Commission. A good example is the investment protection agreement between the EU and China (EU–China Comprehensive Agreement on Investment [CAI]), which was reached at the end of 2020. It improved market access and the level playing field for European companies in China and forced Beijing to make concessions on climate policy and occupational safety standards. However, the European Parliament put the agreement on hold in light of China's sanctions against European lawmakers (China's reaction to the West's Uyghur sanctions). The fate of the EU–China investment protection agreement is therefore uncertain.

However, the EU is also beginning to equip itself against the superpowers' economic coercive measures that are incompatible with the WTO. For example, the EU is in the process of developing a legal basis to deter third-party sanctions (Anti-Coercion Instrument). The US sanctions that have an extraterritorial effect, i.e. that force European companies to follow US legislation, are also being targeted. As a rule, however, the Europeans are not the first to resort to pressure and threats, relying instead on negotiations to avoid economic coercive measures. The EU is currently in dialogue with the Biden administration in an attempt to resolve existing trade disputes. Indeed, in the long-standing dispute between Boeing and Airbus as well as in the transatlantic conflict over the steel and aluminum tariffs imposed by President Trump (on a dubious legal basis), an understanding is in sight. In addition, the establishment of a "Trade and Technology Council" was agreed at the last EU–US summit. This will be an important body that is intended to identify areas of transatlantic common ground in future, for example, on issues concerning 5G/6G infrastructure, semiconductor production, export controls, investment reviews, as well as regulation and standards-setting.

VI. EUROPE'S ROLE IN THE SUPERPOWER CONFLICT

The antagonistic relationship between China and the US threatens to make life difficult for Europe. It would be fatal to get caught in a spiral of conflict from which there is no longer hope of escape. Europe is the last place that would be interested in a new "Cold War 2.0." The attitude towards China threatens to become a litmus test of transatlantic relations as well. As for Germany, equidistance between the US and China cannot be a serious option, because of Germany's strong roots in the transatlantic community intellectually and in terms of security policy and economics. The EU would do well to set up a joint China agenda with the US that describes a differentiated relationship with China in European terms. From a mainly European point of view, China is three things at once: a partner (on global issues such as climate change, nuclear non-proliferation, the fight against terrorism), a competitor (on issues of economy and technology), and an adversary (in the arenas of military security and in cases of China's expansion in violation of international law). It is therefore crucial to calibrate the relationship with China wisely and not rely solely on confrontation, while at the same time not endangering the transatlantic alliance. This requires long-term strategic thinking and statecraft. Positioning the European Union correctly in terms of the superpower rivalry between the US and China will be one of the most important tasks in the future.

Notes

1. Freedom House, Global Freedom Scores, https://freedomhouse.org/countries/freedom-world/scores (accessed November 11, 2021).
2. Economist Intelligence Unit, Democracy Index 2020: "In Sickness and in Health?" EIU 2021, p. 3.

CHAPTER 12

IS THE RISE OF CHINA ENDANGERING OUR FREEDOM?

GABRIEL FELBERMAYR

China's economic and political rise from the world's largest workhouse to one of the largest economic powerhouses in the world is the major geo-strategic event to have taken place after the end of the Cold War. In 1990 China accounted for less than 2 percent of global economic output measured in US dollars, even though China was home to 21 percent of the world's population. In 2020 China's share of global gross domestic product (GDP) rose to over 17 percent, while its share of population fell to 18 percent. In terms of purchasing power, China's proportion of global

GDP is even greater. In 1990, the average purchasing power of a Chinese citizen was about US$980, or about 4 percent of the US equivalent. By 2020 it had risen to over $17,000, or about 27 percent of the US figure. Economically, China is no longer a developing country. China's sheer size makes it one of the three most important power centers in the global economy, alongside the US and the EU. This obviously has a significant impact on the scope for action of individual countries such as Germany.

When the Cold War ended in 1990, people talked about the end of history. In his famous book, Francis Fukuyama said that liberalism had prevailed politically and economically and that totalitarian systems no longer represented an alternative. The liberal principles of basic rights, the rule of law, and the free-market economy would henceforth, he claimed, characterize all global societies.[1] Today it has become clear that this was a Utopian notion. China has achieved its extraordinary rise in blatant disregard for these very principles of freedom. Some people even claim that this is the only way such rapid economic growth was possible.

TAIWAN AND HONG KONG

Consequently, China's success is curtailing the reach of the Western liberal system. Its system of authoritarian state capitalism offers an alternative that is reducing Western influence in third countries from Latin America to Africa and Asia. And as China's global economic power grows, so does the likelihood that the country will be able to expand its concept of statehood. The constant suppression of democracy in Hong Kong or the increasing tensions over Taiwan are concrete examples of this. Clearly, Chinese expansion in this region threatens the freedom of the countries and residents of the "West" (loosely defined here as North America plus Western and Central Europe) as their influence and privileges diminish. If there is an escalation of tensions over Taiwan, there would also be very significant economic consequences: for example, because a large proportion of global semiconductor production would come under direct Chinese control.

China's behavior with regard to Hong Kong or Taiwan is not (only) about the expansion of the specifically Chinese state and social ideology, but rather expresses the highly nationalistic motivation to restore China's territorial conditions and global reputation to its position before the "century of humiliation" (the period between the forced opening of Chinese ports to the British opium trade in 1842 and the founding of the People's Republic in 1949).[2]

Whether such a Chinese resurgence goes hand in hand with a restriction of "our" freedom is an interesting and by no means trivial question. In game theory, it makes sense to distinguish between the logic of positive-sum and zero-sum games. In this case, however, a dynamic view is needed, because there is repeated interaction on the one hand, and on the other short-term losses can be compensated for by longer-term gains and vice versa. In a positive-sum game, it is possible for all participants in a game (i.e. in a strategic interaction) to be absolutely better off at the same time. In a zero-sum game this isn't possible: if one player wins, another always loses. However, because the world comprises many countries, such an analysis based on game-theory is complicated. For example, it is clear that Chinese aggression towards Taiwan or Hong Kong would cost the West a certain amount of freedom; it is quite possible, however, that Beijing acting tough in its own backyard would result in a loss of China's reputation and influence in other regions of the world, and this would strengthen the West's position in the game. In both political and economic terms, it is highly likely that changes will lead to powerful distributive effects, and that an increase in overall prosperity or collective security will be accompanied by a significant decline in welfare and security for individual members of the global community.

It also makes sense to distinguish between collective (state) interests and individual interests. States define their sovereignty as the freedom to make their own political decisions, i.e. not to be at the mercy of external pressures. For individuals, freedom can be defined economically as freedom of choice, i.e. as the possibility of being able to choose freely between alternatives. But it is obvious that it is possible for a government to increase their scope for action, i.e. to experience an increase in freedom, while at the same time individual groups within the state are suffering a loss of freedom. This is not a characteristic of dictatorships alone.

CHINA'S ECONOMIC RISE AND FREEDOM IN THE WEST

If we ignore issues of power politics and focus solely on China's process of growth, the possibility of a positive-sum game becomes apparent. The economists Chang-Tai Hsieh and Ralph Ossa have estimated

China's productivity growth at sector level and used a quantitative model of the global economy to calculate the effects this has had on per capita incomes in various countries around the world. Their study shows that in the period 1995 to 2007 alone, real per capita income in China increased by 230 percent as a result of productivity growth.[3] World income increased by about 8 percent; outside China, real incomes were broadly unchanged. A study by Julian di Giovanni et al. concludes that, on average, there may even have been significant net gains outside of China.[4]

Outside China, admittedly, a high level of heterogeneity is to be expected. To put it simply, two mechanisms can be distinguished that are driven by the change in relative prices on the world markets. It is not surprising that the integration into the global economy of a comparatively poor national economy, which nevertheless comprises around one fifth of the world's population, changes these conditions of exchange significantly. Many goods—from textiles, shoes, electronics, and furniture to industrial intermediate products and machines—have become cheaper due to China's expanded production. Many Western consumers have benefited from the reduction in scarcity. In addition, access to cheaper industrial intermediate products has helped Western producers to achieve lower production costs. On the other hand, however, workers outside China have suffered from increased competition and the relocation of production, losing both income and jobs. It is a matter of quantitative analysis which has the stronger impact. And so it turns out that countries such as India, South Korea, and Japan may have benefited, while others like Canada, Spain, and the United Kingdom have probably lost out. In Germany and the US, the positive and negative forces have pretty much balanced each other out. Overall, however, the effects are small. The changes within the countries are much more serious— China's increase in strength has probably increased economic inequality considerably.[5]

The calculations cited above make it clear that China's economic rise did not happen at the expense of other countries across the board to the extent that we can talk about a positive-sum game. However, the example also shows that outside China some countries became more prosperous while others became less so. These comments refer to national averages that hide significant redistributive effects within countries. Wherever the rise of China has led to higher real incomes, we can talk about an increase in freedom from an economic perspective: people who have more income have more alternatives. This follows the logic of development as freedom as put forward by Amartya Sen, both at the individual and the collective level.[6]

This interpretation of events may seem naive inasmuch as China interacts with other states and their citizens not only in the context of competitively organized markets. For example, competition for market share may be compatible with positive-sum logic, but rivalry for dominance of natural resources is certainly not. In addition, because of the systemic differences between China and the "West," the issue is not just economic power but military and political power as well. In this case, zero-sum logic is dominant, because the crucial question is one of ranking. In keeping with economic welfare theory, the above representation focuses on absolute real incomes: an increase in one's own real purchasing power is synonymous with an increase in one's own freedom. However, it is likely that relative incomes are also relevant, perhaps predominantly so. As long as China's economic power is increasing faster than that of a geo-strategic rival, it becomes increasingly possible that China will use its comparatively greater options to assert its interests—both political and economic—at the expense of the rival, thereby limiting the latter's scope for independent action. In the context of geo-strategic rivalry in particular, a change in the corresponding position and not the absolute level of individual income is relevant to how freely a state can act. The above-mentioned study by Hsieh and Ossa shows in a striking way that China's productivity growth has primarily led to an improvement in its relative economic power.[7]

ECONOMIC CONVERGENCE THROUGH TRADE

China's increase in productivity may have been the result of purely domestic processes that took place independently of other countries. However, it is much more likely that the openness of many rich countries after the founding of the World Trade Organization (WTO) in 1995 created a situation that allowed China to import modern technologies from abroad and make use of them. So it was a conscious act of liberalization by the West that played a major part in enabling China's resurgence. This argument can also be shown through modeling experiments, in which technological conditions remain constant and the effects of trade liberalization alone are assessed. Julian di Giovanni et al. show that China's participation in world trade has enabled China to achieve significantly larger gains in real per capita income than most other countries.[8] In most models this is partly a natural outcome of the international division of labor: when a poor and a rich country start trading with one another, they make trading profits which, in absolute terms, are often of a similar magnitude. For the poor country, however, this means growth that is relatively greater than that of the rich country. This is to be expected especially when the countries in question are large, which is the case in China. In other words, trade liberalization led to a convergence of per capita incomes in China and the West. While China's accession to the WTO also brought overall gains in welfare in the US or Europe, the percentage increase was larger in China. China's relative position improved.

In addition, from about 2005, that is around five years after China joined the World Trade Organization, Beijing abandoned its unilateral efforts to open up the country further. Instead, it pursued a strategy of import substitution: according to the OECD, in 2005 one US dollar was worth around 26 US cents in export value, i.e. around a quarter of added value in export terms. This value has now fallen to less than 15 percent. This means that China's openness has declined significantly, while China's proportion of world trade has increased. So in addition to the country becoming stronger compared with others, there has also been a reduction in dependency on foreign countries, both developments taking place in a short period of time and on a quantitatively considerable scale.

In a world without system rivalry, shifting relative positions could easily be dismissed. The economic resurgence of Europe after World War II meant a rapid relative improvement by comparison with the United States; but the absence of deep political divisions, that is the United States' clearly dominant position, made this fact seem insignificant. Japan's process of catch-up, which took place somewhat later, was regarded a little more critically in the US, although there was no system rivalry in this case either. The West's relationship with China is different.

POLITICIZATION OF ECONOMIC INTERDEPENDENCE; ECONOMIZATION OF POLITICS

In recent years, it has become clear that China is using its increasing economic power for political ends and, conversely, using political pressure to achieve economic goals. A situation in which economic and political power are closely intertwined and interdependent is nothing new. But the fact that a former developing country is using this toolkit and doing so very skillfully is quite a novel experience. A central vehicle by which China exerts political influence through economic policy are foreign investments in the context of the New Silk Road.[9]

China has also used the opportunities offered by the WTO very well to its own advantage. For example, for many years it has manipulated its own currency's exchange rate relative to the dollar and Euro to generate export surpluses, which China has used to build up foreign exchange reserves and invest in other foreign assets. The rules of the World Trade Organization offer no way of combating this. Even subsidizing companies using low-interest loans, for example, was almost impossible for the WTO to sanction. The massive use of so-called anti-dumping procedures by the EU or the US against China is a reaction to such distorted competition.

The accusation often leveled against China is that the country is trying to gain market share through unfair means in order to achieve market-dominant positions and profit from such monopolies. In fact, the essence of state capitalism is the state using its powers to influence economic outcomes and, conversely, politically exploiting economic dependencies. If a country has no separation between the political and economic spheres, then the free movement of goods and capital with that country contains the risk that trading partners can be strategically outmaneuvered.

TECHNOLOGICAL DOMINANCE

In the last few years, issues of economic dominance and the regulation of new technologies have become crucial. For example, China operates with different premises when it comes to regulating data, and the country lends differing weight to individual versus state interests. In the global economy, there is often little point in applying different standards in different jurisdictions to technologies on which internationally traded goods depend. Countries are therefore trying to establish their own standards as internationally as possible, either by having their trading partners adopt or at least recognize their standards to gain market access. This gives national companies clear advantages in international competition, because often only a single standard can prevail. This is a zero-sum game: if China sets a global standard, then the EU or the US cannot do so at the same time. The size of the domestic market is particularly relevant when it comes to having the power to enforce standards. This is another reason why countries worry about the relative size of their economies. The EU integration process aims to create a large internal market that will give EU regulation a significant home advantage. Anu Bradford, an expert in international trade law, has dubbed this the "Brussels effect"[10] and she shows that the EU has been successful in doing this in the past. It is not surprising that China too is pursuing this strategy. By self-confidently setting standards, the Chinese are restricting Europe's room for maneuver and thus Europe's freedom, even if it has positive effects on the economic success of individual European companies.

The debate about the future regulation of self-driving vehicles is a good example of this. The question is whether the vehicles themselves or the infrastructure should be intelligent. Are the individual vehicles actively steering themselves, or are they connected to a collective system that does the steering? The West is certainly more inclined towards a decentralized system; China to a centralized one. As China is the world's largest car market, the country has considerable influence over which standard will prevail.

DECOUPLING

The global economy is more interconnected than ever in human history. The world has come closer to the ideal of a single market than it ever has been in the past as a result of falling physical transport costs, falling communication costs, multilateral and regional trade agreements, the emergence of multinational corporations, and the high level of mobility of people, ideas, and capital across borders. However, this close interconnectedness means that changes in one part of the world can lead to distortions in another part. And when one part of the world uses political means to manipulate market activity in order to gain power, the other part of the world must respond in order not to lose power.

Countries or regions with incompatible political systems could evade this kind of complex interaction by closing off their markets, and this indeed happened for long periods of postwar history when the communist region of the world had only limited trade with the "West." There was no global economy, but instead two systems existed side by side. Each system was thus able to preserve its internal integrity.

But decoupling, i.e. reducing economic interdependence, would entail high costs. The price would be a lower level of prosperity, a reduced ability to innovate, and most importantly, a reduced ability to deal with common global threats such as climate change. Furthermore, it is far from clear that less political integration reduces the likelihood of political or even military conflict; we might instead assume the opposite.[11]

WHAT CAN EUROPE DO?

The European Union is increasingly facing up to the challenges posed by the rise of China—and perhaps other countries in the future. It has launched a new strategy of "open, sustainable, and assertive trade policy" and is now trying to implement it. To this end, new regulations are being developed, which are to be decisively promoted under France's EU Council presidency, beginning in January 2022. There is a lot at stake, especially for the German economy. The Commission is determined to learn the language of power by further developing the tools of trade policy. Almost inevitably it comes down to the details. The European Union is currently working on new rules for common external trade policy. For example, regulations on international procurement, protection against economic coercion, and a carbon border adjustment system are in preparation. The EU also wants to introduce an EU-wide supply chain law.

These measures are bringing fundamental changes to the EU's external trade policy, politicizing it and using it for various geo-strategic goals. This means adjusting and expanding the range of instruments, but also harbors the risk of an increase in protectionism. Paradoxically, new defensive instruments are needed that can hold out the prospect of sanctions in order to punish breaches of the law credibly, demand reciprocity effectively, and thus ensure the stability of the world trade system. But it is important not to lose sight of the goal of open markets, otherwise the EU, together with its trading partners, may find itself in a zero-sum game in which economic freedoms are shrinking on all sides, in both formal and material terms.

Notes

1. Francis Fukuyama, *The End of History and the Last Man* (New York: Penguin, 1992).
2. Klaus Mühlhahn, *Making China Modern: From the Great Qing to Xi Jinping* (Cambridge, MA: The Belknap Press of Harvard University Press, 2019).

3. Chang-Tai Hsieh and Ralph Ossa, "A Global View of Productivity Growth in China" in *Journal of International Economics* 102(C), 2016, pp. 209–224.

4. Julian di Giovanni, Andrei Levchenko, and Jing Zhang, "The Global Welfare Impact of China: Trade Integration and Technological Change" in *American Economic Journal: Macroeconomics* 6(3), 2014, pp. 153–183.

5. See, for example, the survey by David Autor, David Dorn, and Gordon Hanson, "The China Shock: Learning from Labor-Market Adjustment to Large Changes in Trade" in *Annual Review of Economics* 8, 2016, pp. 205–240.

6. See Amartya Sen, *Development as Freedom* (New York: Oxford University Press, 1999).

7. Hsieh and Ossa, "A Global View of Productivity Growth in China."

8. Di Giovanni et al., "The Global Welfare Impact of China."

9. See Gabriel Felbermayr, Alexander Sandkamp, Wan-Hsin Liu, Frank Bickenbach, and Moritz Goldbeck, "Megatrends im Welthandel: Die neue Seidenstraße – Wachstumsregion zwischen Europa und Asien" ifo Studie commissioned by IHK for Munich and Upper Bavaria, 2019.

10. Anu Bradford, *The Brussels Effect: How the European Union Rules the World* (New York: Oxford University Press, 2020).

11. See Philippe Martin, Thierry Mayer, and Mathias Thoenig, "Make Trade not War?" in *Review of Economic Studies* 75, 2008, pp. 865–900.

CHAPTER 13

THE EUROPEAN MODEL OF FREEDOM IN SYSTEM CONFLICT: UNDER STRESS AND PUT TO THE TEST

SVEN SIMON

I. SYSTEMIC COMPETITION AS A TEST FOR FREEDOM AND DEMOCRACY

In spring 2019, the European Commission published a strategy paper on the future of EU–China relations.[1] This paper represents a paradigm shift in the geopolitical orientation of the European Union. In it, the Commission characterizes the People's Republic of China not only as an "economic competitor" but also for the first time as a "systemic rival" promoting "alternative models of governance." According to the Commission, Chinese investments are threatening socio-economic and financial sustainability as well as the rule of law and good governance in Africa, in non-EU Europe, and increasingly also in Member States of the European Union.

Two decades after China joined the World Trade Organization, many predictions about an irreversible rapprochement between the People's Republic and the "Western" model of liberal democracy have not come true. Francis Fukuyama's much-cited prediction of the "end of history" did not materialize.[2] Instead of enjoying a hegemony of liberalism and democracy, Europeans find themselves at the beginning of the third decade of the 21st century in a systemic conflict with an autocratic political model, as currently operating in China. Unlike the Cold War of the previous century, today's systemic competition—at least currently and from a European perspective—is not a dispute about military dominance. Rather, it is about economic prosperity, leadership in global technology, and success in overcoming social challenges and natural threats. The measure of success of this global system conflict is what political scientists call "output legitimation."[3]

Which system is better able to deliver on its promise of prosperity; which system can deal more effectively with the major challenges of today?

On these terms, politics is measured against concrete results and in a global context. It also puts the system of liberal democracy under pressure to prove itself, and it means that liberal democracy is no longer beyond comparison with other systems. The fact that China has been seeking this competition for decades and is pursuing a long-term plan is clearly evident in Africa and also in China's New Silk Road initiative. Germany's then Minister of Foreign Affairs and Vice-Chancellor Sigmar Gabriel rightly pointed this out at the Munich Security Conference in 2018:

> The initiative for a new Silk Road is not what some people in Germany believe it to be—it is not a sentimental nod to Marco Polo, but rather stands for an attempt to establish a comprehensive system to shape the world according to China's interests. This has long since ceased to be merely a question of economics. China is developing a comprehensive systemic alternative to the Western model that, in contrast to our own, is not founded on freedom, democracy, and individual human rights.[4]

This is a new development for us. For over 300 years the Western world has exerted its influence, first through colonization, then through globalization. All global economic standards, all institutions and organizations, the international legal system, human rights—they are all Western in character. This era is over. Annual growth rates of over 8 percent ensure that other parts of the world are catching up. At the start of the 20th century, 20 percent of the world's population was European. Today it is 6 percent;[5] in 2050 the proportion will be around 5 percent. At the same time, the African continent is growing by a million people every week.[6] And economically, the future is often happening elsewhere. Today Europe's share of global gross national product is only 20 percent; 90 percent of global growth is taking place outside Europe.[7] In the digital economy, Europe is completely left behind. The world has been decisively carved up between Google, Apple, Facebook, and Amazon in the West; and by Samsung, Huawei, Tencent, and Alibaba in the East.

The European Union is still one of the world's largest economic areas and has political clout. Our values of individual freedom, the rule of law, and democracy are still attractive, but our model lost its unchallenged status some time ago. Up-and-coming new powers are claiming economic and political influence, and China in particular is competing with the West on its promise of prosperity. The successes and failures involved in dealing with the COVID-19 pandemic can be seen as the current chapter in this systemic competition. We need to ask what the effects will be on our self-image as a free and democratic society if public life in China's one-party state seems to be returning to normal quicker than in Europe. Germany's President Frank-Walter Steinmeier expressed this uncertainty very elegantly in a nutshell: "Declines in growth can be compensated for; damage to one's self-image heals less easily."[8] The idea that an authoritarian one-party state could be superior to us in aspects of governance poses a challenge to our self-image. In particular, it questions a widespread attitude in Europe that the political actions of the West are still the only benchmark on the world stage. Many people in Africa have long since stopped believing that.

II. PROTECTING FREEDOM AND DEMOCRACY BY CREATING AN EU FOR THE 21ST CENTURY

For societies based on freedom, a system conflict with authoritarian states such as China poses a particular challenge, because social resources are not simply at the disposal of their state authorities. The self-imposed limitations of democratic systems necessarily reduce their ability to take action.[9] Totalitarian states are much less subject to questioning on such matters. In a global systemic competition, systems such as the Chinese one-party state always have the advantage of more extensive spheres of action, the ability to disengage themselves from legal processes, and far fewer limitations on their opportunities to intervene. By contrast, a constitutional state has legal obligations and adherence to procedure, and takes time to enact democratic processes. Against the backdrop of these challenges, the question arises as to which course a united Europe should take in the 21st century. I advocate two fundamental policy decisions. First, we in Europe have to be certain of ourselves—we have to redefine the need for the European Union in the 21st century, and explain it to everyone. Second, to do this, we must embark on a course of reform that enhances Europe's ability to act without calling into question our basic values of the rule of law, democracy, and freedom of the individual.

When the European Coal and Steel Community was founded by Robert Schuman and Jean Monnet in 1952, the guiding promise of European integration was peace, freedom, and shared prosperity. These values are still right and important, and in no way should they be taken for granted. At the same time, to a generation for whom war in Europe fortunately seems unthinkable, peace is a very abstract concept. That is why we need a new narrative for European integration—a paradigm shift from internal to global orientation. The states of Europe founded the European Union as protection *against* one another, now it must be developed further as a means of protection *for* one another. In this respect, today it is not an abstract question of more or less Europe, and certainly not about old ideas of a federal system, nor is it a question of the old dispute about the EU's constitutional purpose. It is about what Europeans need the European Union for in the 21st century: they need it in order to be able to assert themselves, as a European group, in a world of superpowers operating unilaterally, with which no European state on their own can compete. They need it in order to be able to provide an effective answer to the serious challenges of the present such as climate change, the migration crisis, digitalization, and shared security. And above all, they need it to be able to defend the European model of freedom in the global system conflict. This is where the real test lies. The European Union represents the only body of the magnitude that can realistically find an answer to these challenges. Either Europeans tackle these challenges together or not at all.

To do this, however, it must be possible to form a unity internally and to be able to act externally. In other words, the test is proving that the supranational model of government is better able to withstand the stress tests of freedom and democracy than each country would be alone. However, if we fall behind on the crucial issues, if we concentrate too much on divisive issues in Brussels, then this will not succeed. Because, unlike the nation state, in the eyes of most contemporaries, the EU is not an end in itself. It is up for grabs, having to prove its *raison d'être* and test itself over and over again in order to survive. The tool that we need to defend the European model of freedom will be measured in terms of costs and benefits. As Brexit has shown, giving due consideration to this is not necessarily a rational process, but it is a reality. If the European Union is to guarantee our European model of freedom, it must make its case once more and concentrate on the essentials. We should transfer powers to the European Union in all areas where joint European cooperation brings concrete and visible added value. This applies to the areas of trade and investment protection abroad and in Europe, security and defense, climate and energy, digitalization, research, and innovation. Linked to this are questions of the internal market and the stabilization of the common currency. In areas in which the nation states have considerable differences in standards, such as in health and social policy, communitization will lead to division for the foreseeable future.

Ultimately, we must improve our performance in the area in which we are fundamentally superior to other systems: free competition of opinions. The democratic process may take longer than decision-making in an autocratic state, but in the end, our system of competition leads to greater efficiency, because wrong decisions can be identified and corrected and majority decisions are more widely accepted. We allow open criticism, and as a result our institutions are more stable in the long term. We impose checks and balances on our governments, and as a result they have to take responsibility, otherwise they will be voted out of office. However, it is precisely in the context of this central competitive advantage of the European or Western model that we have our shortcomings and a lot of catching up to do at the European level. Often, the greatest challenge is to communicate political decisions. In a democracy, this is part of being able to promote the necessary acceptance of decisions. However, in Europe this kind of communication is by and large not happening. The problem starts with the lack of a European public sphere. Instead, we are dealing with a highly fragmented political debate that is being conducted in 27 different parts of the public sphere. Then there are the language barriers and the internal organization of the European Parliament. Most of the plenary debates are not worthy of the name; instead, MEPs make one-minute statements in their mother tongue. A real debate in the sense of a publicly understood exchange is not taking place, which means that a core element of democratic legitimation is missing.

Highly political decisions at the European level are thus made in a kind of non-political sphere with no explanation. This has been corroding the acceptance of European integration over the past few years. Another central problem is the diffusion of responsibility that takes place at the European level. This became clear when questions were asked about the procurement of vaccines. Very few people know which institution is responsible for which tasks, which makes it particularly easy to complain about the EU as a whole. Linked to this is the lack of responsiveness, as political science describes the phenomenon describing the various aspects of politicians' willingness to respond to the interests of citizens. It starts with the European elections, which give voters the impression that nothing will change after the elections anyway. In the past there were grand coalitions, today we have a very grand, pro-European coalition countering a group of anti-Europeans, which makes majorities and minorities indistinguishable. The Commission is staffed by the governments of the Member States. It is true that the Parliament has some influence on its composition at the beginning of the legislative period, but the central element of democracy, namely the ability to elect and vote out a government, is missing. Added to this is the fact that EU law is difficult to change and, finally, that Parliament lacks the right of initiative, not so much concerning new legislation, but when it comes to changing existing rules.

Most people are not aware of this in such great detail. But of course they can see that their expectations of the EU are not being met. If the European Union is to defend freedom and democracy, we need a real competition of opinions at European level, a shared public sphere, and a focus on those issues where European cooperation brings concrete and visible added value. Even then it remains difficult, since added value is not always the same for everyone, because common European interests are not always the sum of the interests of the Member States.

III. OUTLOOK

The next few years will see a critical phase in which the course will be set for the future of Europe and for the competition between systems. Compared with the era of Robert Schuman, the focus today is on the paradigm shift from internal to global orientation we described above. Hand in hand with the "creation of an ever-closer union" internally, a union capable of action must operate externally. It is important that we eliminate the shortcomings described, which exist in Europe in precisely those areas where our Western model has the decisive competitive advantage. The conference on the future of Europe, which has been taking place since May 9, 2021, is an opportunity to shape a focused, effective, and democratic Union that anchors firmly at European level the strengths of our European model of freedom, the competition of opinions in the deliberative process, greater efficiency, greater acceptance, and a more stable system in the long term. If this succeeds, it will be possible to successfully defend the European model of freedom in a global system conflict. Compared with the courage of the generation 70 years ago, who reached out in reconciliation to their former wartime enemies over the ruins of Europe's cities, today's challenges are not overly ambitious.

Notes

1. Joint Communication to the European Parliament, the European Council and the Council, JOIN(2019) 5 final, March 12, 2019, https://ec.europa.eu/info/sites/default/files/communication-eu-china-a-strategic-outlook.pdf (accessed November 22, 2021).
2. Francis Fukuyama, "The End of History?" in *The National Interest* 16, 1989, pp. 3–18, http://www.jstor.org/stable/24027184 (accessed November 22, 2021).
3. On the concept of output legitimation see Fritz Scharpf, "Legitimationskonzepte jenseits des Nationalstaats" in MPIfG Working Paper 04/6, November 2004, https://pure.mpg.de/rest/items/item_1234256_12/component/file_3315564/content (accessed November 22, 2021).
4. Sigmar Gabriel, Munich Security Conference, February 17, 2018, https://www.auswaertiges-amt.de/en/newsroom/news/rede-muenchner-sicherheitskonferenz/1602662 (accessed November 22, 2021).
5. Eurostat, "A Statistical Portrait of the European Union compared with G20 Countries," press release, https://ec.europa.eu/eurostat/documents/2995521/10928892/1-02062020-AP-EN.pdf/c3253596-bbda-491e-6f59-62a7e5f5c965 (accessed November 22, 2021).
6. Federal Institute for Population Research, "Bevölkerungszahl und ihr Wachstum, Afrika (1950-2020)", https://www.bib.bund.de/DE/Fakten/Fakt/

W24-Bevoelkerungszahl-Wachstum-Afrika-ab-1950.html (accessed November 22, 2021).

7. Statista, "Europäische Union: Anteil am kaufkraftbereinigten globalen Bruttosozialprodukt (BIP) von 1980 bis 2020 und Prognosen bis 2016", https://de.statista.com/statistik/daten/studie/249045/umfrage/anteil-der-europaeischen-union-eu-am-globalen-bruttoinlandsprodukt-bip/ (accessed November 22, 2021).

8. Frank-Walter Steinmeier, byline article in *Merkur* magazine, March 25, 2021, https://www.bundespraesident.de/SharedDocs/Reden/DE/Frank-Walter-Steinmeier/Zeitungsbeitraege/2021/210325-Merkur-Namensbeitrag.html (accessed November 22, 2021).

9. Frank Schale and Ellen Thümmler, "Den totalitären Staat denken" in *Den totalitären Staat denken*, ed. Frank Schale and Ellen Thümmler (Baden-Baden: Nomos, 2015), pp. 9–28, https://www.nomos-elibrary.de/10.5771/9783845256801-9/den-totalitaeren-staat-denken (accessed November 22, 2021).

CHAPTER 14

FREEDOM, EQUALITY, DEMOCRACY

CLAUDIA WIESNER

INTRODUCTION

In this essay I will be discussing the relationship between the two dimensions of freedom and equality in representative democracies. Basically, we can say that representative democracy must always combine both dimensions in equal value and in relation to each other—this follows from the basic idea of democracy as government of the people, by the people, and for the people.[1] The people—the democratic sovereign or the demos—must govern itself, and this self-government is based on the principles of freedom and equality. In representative democracies, these dimensions are implemented through institutions, processes, and rights.

For self-government to be implemented substantively, it must first be based on equality. Democratic equality means first of all the equality of members of the demos, the democratic sovereign. In representative democracies this means that each member has one vote, which is given equal weight in elections; every member has the same rights of participation and freedom; every member is equal before the law. On the other hand, self-government also requires freedom: the freedom to decide, at least in elections; and the freedom to participate in government of the people, with the people, and by the people. In representative democracies, democratic freedom is defined in terms of civil and political freedom. In Western democracies the catalogues of rights include, among other things, the right to freedom of expression; free elections; freedom of assembly, association, and protest; freedom to choose one's profession, sexual orientation, religion, and coexistence. Ultimately, these rights to freedom and equality are closely linked to the status of citizens. Non-members of the democratic sovereign, i.e. persons lacking the relevant citizenship, do not enjoy rights to democratic freedom and equality in the same way.

In the following essay, I will first discuss the relationship between freedom and equality in representative democracies in terms of institutions, processes, rights, and obligations. I will then examine three areas where these principles currently need to be brought into balance, namely the pandemic, the question of how to deal with difference, and the role of social rights.

FREEDOM, EQUALITY, AND THE INSTITUTIONS AND PROCESSES OF REPRESENTATIVE DEMOCRACY

There is no such thing as the quintessential democracy, or even the quintessential representative democracy. Rather, different types of democracy of differing quality and with different characteristics are to be found throughout the world. Accordingly, political systems research makes a distinction not just between presidential, semi-presidential, and parliamentary democracies, but also between democracies and autocracies and, even more precisely, between liberal democracies, defective democracies, and autocracies.[2]

Representative democracy is underpinned by institutions and processes; studies of democracy offer different interpretations of which institutions and processes are essential in this. Current definitions of democracy are, for example, the electoral democracy that the research institute Freedom House was evaluating up until 2020, which identifies the following structures of representative democracy:[3]

1. a competitive multi-party system;
2. universal suffrage for all adult citizens;
3. regular elections that are free from electoral fraud and which are a representative reflection of public opinion;
4. the opportunity to address the electorate (voters) through the media and open political campaigns.

The political sociologist Larry Diamond and the political scientist Leonardo Morlino have defined eight dimensions of democracy:[4]

1. rule of law;
2. participation;
3. competition;
4. vertical accountability (politicians can be made responsible by voters and then re-elected or voted out of office);

5. horizontal accountability (for example a mutual balance of power between different institutions);
6. freedom;
7. equality;
8. responsiveness (politicians are prepared to tackle issues that are important to voters).

The model of "embedded democracy" is structured in a similar way to that of Diamond and Morlino.[5] It defines the core of representative democracy as:
1. the electoral regime (or electoral democracy as defined by Freedom House) and emphasizes that for this to function, the following are required:
2. political rights
3. civil rights
4. horizontal accountability
5. the effective power to govern.

More recent research into democracy identifies a core of representative democracy that can be described as electoral regime. This requires freedom (of competition and participation) and equality (of voting weights and rights of participation) in order to function. The electoral regime is complemented by two central dimensions: the constitutional structures that enact freedom and equality in institutions and democratic processes and that guarantee accountability; and the political and civil rights that realize democratic freedom and equality for the individual.

Democracy indices and barometers of civil liberties such as V-Dem and Freedom House differentiate these features by means of scales and then classify the systems as particularly successful democracies or particularly free states according to their respective scores. For example, in the V-Dem Index, which measures liberal democracy (the ranking here ranges from 0 for not democratic, to 1 for democratic), the Federal Republic of Germany has been continuously classified on a range of at least 0.8 since the state's foundation: in 2020 it was 0.83. To cite Turkey in comparison, here V-Dem reveals sharp fluctuations since the end of World War II and a real decline since 2004, when Turkey still managed 0.53 points on the V-Dem index, while since 2020 it has only attained 0.11.[6] Freedom House's ranking focuses more on democratic and civil liberties. With very similar results to the V-Dem Index, this shows that these freedoms are closely linked to the quality of democracy. In 2020 Germany's Freedom House score was 94 out of a possible 100 points, while Sweden scored 100 out of 100. Turkey scored just 32 out of 100 points and is therefore rated by Freedom House as "not free". Ultimately, Freedom House offers its main conclusion: for about 15 years, we have seen an erosion of representative democracies throughout the world.[7]

THE INSTITUTIONALIZATION OF FREEDOM AND EQUALITY: CITIZENSHIP AND DEMOCRACY

In representative democracies, rights to freedom and equality are closely linked to a citizen's status.[8] Non-citizens are not entitled to such rights to the same extent. Drawing on the sociologists T.H. Marshall's and Charles Tilly's classic definitions, citizenship means *the formalized and practical relationship between a polity and its members.*[9] The concept refers to the conditions of this relationship, its institutionalization, and its practical configuration.

Citizenship is thus a central category for modern democracies: in the first place it defines, both legally and formally, the democratic sovereign, the *demos*, using *membership criteria*. Its members usually have rights that are guaranteed by the *polity* (the political system of institutions), but also through their obligations to the polity, such as military service, compulsory schooling, or tax liabilities. Civil liberties are therefore linked to obligations towards the community of citizens and the state, and these obligations in turn limit civil liberties. As Marshall describes, civil rights emerged historically one after the other, and mostly have been fought for politically.[10] Civil liberties were followed by political rights and ultimately social rights. Rights to self-determination in terms of culture and identity, and rights to equality of treatment can be regarded as the latest generation of rights. Finally, political participation is another element of citizenship.

This means that we can distinguish four different aspects of citizenship: the *conditions*, the legal consequences in terms of *rights* and *obligations*, and the *active configuration* of membership of a *polity*. Membership criteria, rights, obligations, and active citizenship form a civic *acquis* [body of acquired rights and obligations] that has developed over centuries, not least through the struggles of the (yet to be recognized) citizens themselves. With regard to the sustainability of democratic life, all these elements are interrelated and interdependent. Rights create the legal basis for the implementation of civil liberties, equality, and democratic participation between citizens and for citizens. However, democratic decision-making systems only work if a *demos* not only has rights and obligations, but also actively fulfils them, i.e. takes part in elections and is politically active.

Finally, historically citizenship is linked to the nation state in two ways. It first emerged in the course of the development of nation states, and therefore the civic *acquis* is related to citizenship of the nation state. With European integration, citizenship became European and Europeanized at the same time. This observation describes a development that has quite ambivalent consequences: in the EU's civic multi-level system, the relationships between citizens, *polity*, and the national elements of citizenship are changing. Membership criteria, rights, obligations, and active citizenship are shifting in their levels of reference, substance, and practical implementation. New rights are being added at EU level, but at the level of the nation state existing rights, especially social rights, are limited in scope.[11]

PANDEMIC, DEMOCRACY, AND FREEDOM

The pandemic entailed a raft of difficult impositions (as then German Chancellor Merkel put it in 2020) on democracy. All over the world, not just in the EU, fundamental rights as well as elementary structures and processes of representative democracy have been suspended. In particular, freedoms have been curtailed by the imposition of curfews, lockdowns, restrictions to freedom of travel, and the obligation to wear a mask. These restrictions to democratic freedom can be justified with two concepts. First, the concept of the state of emergency which justifies special state interventions in order to protect the common good in an emergency. Second, well-founded trade-offs were made between conflicting legal interests. In the pandemic, for example, there are contradictions between the fundamental right to life, physical integrity, and civil liberties. The freedom of the individual to visit restaurants while unvaccinated, to move freely, or to cross borders, was or is being restricted in the pandemic in order to protect the majority of the population and to avoid overwhelming hospitals and ultimately making choices between patients. In this context, the obligation to wear masks in public seems a minor encroachment on individual freedom, as masks have been shown to reduce the general risk of infection considerably and thus protect the rights to life and physical integrity of the majority of the population as a whole. But the right to education has also been curtailed to a very considerable extent, as a result of the months of school closures. At the same time, a civic obligation, namely compulsory schooling, has been suspended.

How can we assess these restrictions to freedom and democracy during the pandemic? From my point of view as a democracy researcher, restricting freedoms during a pandemic is inevitable, because the common good and the right to life fundamentally require and justify it. However, it is questionable whether and for how long these restrictions were justified in each case. For example, all other EU countries allowed schools to stay open longer than Germany, which emphasizes the fact that legally protected rights are accorded different importance in different cultures. More worrying than the restriction on rights of freedom is the fact that during the pandemic almost everywhere in Europe including in the Federal Republic of Germany decisions were made primarily by the executive. If the German Chancellor and the Ministerial Conference of Federal States, and not the Bundestag, are deciding what the pandemic rules will look like, the Bundestag is being disempowered to a certain extent.

DEMOCRATIC FREEDOM AND DIFFERENCE

Another current challenge for freedom and equality in representative democracies is the issue of marrying these principles with individual and group rights, since democratic equality does not mean that people are actually all the same. Individuals are different. A catalogue of rights that is blind to differences is based on a Utopian aspiration to an abstract, uniform individual. Representative democracies are thus faced with the challenge of making differences of, for example, culture, gender, or origin coherent with individuals' alignment with the political community of citizens.[12]

This demand is neither simple nor uncomplicated in its implementation. Today, in many Western democracies, dealing with difference harbors considerable potential for conflict. It is always a question of which role we give to which understanding of freedom and equality. This is illustrated in the debate about teachers in German schools wearing the headscarf. For example, a devout Muslim woman schoolteacher wanted to wear the headscarf in school. She asserted her right to the free practice of religion and free development of personality. Her employer, the state of Baden-Württemberg, argued against this, saying that the headscarf is not just a religious symbol but also a political one, and thus violates the principle of neutrality that applies to the work of teachers as representatives of the state.

The example highlights various conflicts—between the individual right to freedom to practice religion, the question of how to evaluate the associated symbols (are they religious or political?), and the politically defined common foundations of democratic schooling and community (ideological neutrality). Is the headscarf a sign of an individual's faith, is it a religious or a political symbol? Are religious symbols treated equally, such as the habit of a nun who works in a school and the headscarf? Should the right to exercise one's religion freely be accorded more importance than the state's religious neutrality? Is it justified to regard a headscarf as a political symbol? In this essay, we cannot and should not discuss this example in depth, but it does illustrate the multitude of possible tensions that can result from the practical implementation of the imperatives of democratic freedom and equality when it comes to dealing with difference. A glance at social media provides enough evidence that a multitude of similar conflicts exist.

But what is the consequence for a society that is extremely heterogeneous in terms of its diversity of languages, identities, and values, and in its ethnic and cultural groups? If these diverse models of identity and value are to be balanced, a common denominator must be found that provides a minimum of democratic consensus alongside the greatest possible acceptance of difference. Differences in ethnic, cultural, or group-related identifications must therefore be accepted, but in turn they must not be so broad that no common core of basic political and democratic values remains. In short, individual freedom must be restricted where it curtails the structure and functioning of democracy.

DEMOCRATIC EQUALITY AND SOCIAL RIGHTS

A third challenge for democracy today is dealing with social inequality. In the "societies of the two-thirds" that are to be found in the majority of current representative democracies, social differences are leading to striking divergences in democratic participation and elections.[13] For example, politics is given more legitimacy by the better-off, while conversely, poorer citizens not only increasingly feel socially left behind, they also do not see themselves recognized as part of democratic society and its processes.[14] However, democratic equality consists primarily in the political equality of the members of the demos, the democratic sovereign. Every member has an equal vote in elections, the same rights of participation and freedom, and is equal before the law. The democratic divides we see in a "two-thirds society" are therefore endangering democratic equality.

Democratic participation that is equal or at least equal before the law presupposes a certain freedom from the most urgent existential concerns and a minimum degree of equality in the conditions of participation. Formal or legal equality alone is not enough; a certain degree of social equality or social justice is also required—as Marshall puts it, "[...] to remove inequalities which cannot be regarded as legitimate."[15] Democracy is, to this extent, dependent on the material guarantee of basic rights to participation in society (the extent of which may be controversial), as the imperatives of free and equal participation in democratic life can only be put into practice if basic material differences and structural obstacles do not restrict them unduly. Otherwise, material deprivation too easily leads to social exclusion and a lack of political participation. The implementation of democratic equality therefore requires the guarantee of certain social rights, which serve, among other things, to minimize structural lacks of freedom and inequalities among the members of the *demos* in order to make the prerequisites for participation not unduly unequal. If we pursue this argument, social rights are necessary for democracy. Because of this connection between legal equality and material equality, Marshall continues, the institution of citizenship leads to the minimization of the social inequality created by the capitalist economic system.[16]

At this point we cannot and should not explore to what extent and in what specific form social rights are necessary for democracy. This is because the way in which the imperative of democratic equality is specifically designed depends a) on the different normative starting positions of those adjudicating and the decision-makers, and b) on the specific form these positions take in their respective political systems (for example, in this respect the political culture of the US is structured differently from most European countries). Basically, we can say that equality should either remain primarily restricted to formal and legal aspects or that it can be materially fulfilled and promoted. In each case, the preferences of the *demos* decide how much inequality is legitimately acceptable.[17]

The context described above is important for representative democracy. Democracy needs the acknowledgment and implementation of social rights, and these in turn require redistribution. The money that the state and its institutions use to reduce structural inequalities must first be collected. The realization of social rights therefore depends on the state collecting enough taxes. In this context, the freedom of the individual is restricted in favor of equality and democracy, and above all the common good.

CONCLUSION

Freedom and equality are fundamental and interrelated dimensions of representative democracy. They are implemented through the institutions, processes, and rights of representative democracies, in which freedom and equality enact a complex interrelationship. For example, there are always conflicts between legally protected rights and between different interests. In the pandemic, civil liberties occupied and still occupy a position of tension vis-à-vis the state of emergency and the right to life. In dealing with difference, the requirement to guarantee citizens' democratic equality comes up against the demand for group rights. In the civic *acquis* [body of acquired rights and obligations], social rights ultimately serve to establish a legal and material basis for the realization of democratic freedom and equality. Full democratic equality cannot be achieved without redistribution.

Overall, we can say that freedom and equality in democracies are not only mutually dependent, but also mutually restrictive. Democracy needs freedom, but this must go hand in hand with the common good and democratic equality. Democratic equality, in turn, requires freedom. Political and democratic rights are mutually dependent and mutually reinforcing, but they are not all equally feasible and can also be in conflict. Freedom, equality, and democracy therefore always appear in new configurations and have to be balanced according to a variety of different normative and political decisions.

Notes

1. Abraham Lincoln, *The Gettysburg Address*, 1863, https://www.pbs.org/newshour/extra/app/uploads/2013/11/Transcript-of-the-Gettysburg-Address.pdf (accessed November 9, 2011).

2. On the difference between presidential, semi-presidential, and parliamentary democracies, see Winfried Steffani, *Parlamentarische und präsidentielle Demokratie: Strukturelle Aspekte westlicher Demokratien* (Opladen: VS Verlag für Sozialwissenschaften, 1979). On the difference between democracies and autarkies, see Juan J. Linz, *Totalitarian and Authoritarian Regimes* (Boulder, CO and London: Lynne Rienner Publishers Inc., 2000); and for more detail, see Wolfgang Merkel, "Embedded and Defective Democracies" in *Democratization* 11 (5), 2004, pp. 33–58.

3. Freedom House, FAQs, https://freedomhouse.org/reports/freedom-world/faq-freedom-world#ElectoralDemocracy (accessed November 1, 2021).

4. Larry Jay Diamond and Leonardo Morlino, "The Quality of Democracy. An Overview" in *Journal of Democracy* 15 (4), 2004, pp. 20-31.

5. See Merkel, "Embedded and Defective Democracies."

6. For all data, see V-Dem, "Liberal Democracy Index 2020", https://ourworldindata.org/grapher/v-dem-liberal-democracy-index (accessed November 1, 2021).

7. For all data, see Freedom House, "Freedom in the World 2020 – Map of Freedom", https://freedomhouse.org/explore-the-map?type=fiw&year=2021 (accessed November 1, 2021).

8. On the following, see Claudia Wiesner, *Bürgerschaft und Demokratie in der EU* (Münster: Lit, 2007); Wiesner, "Women's Partial Citizenship" in *The Ashgate Research Companion to the Politics of Democratization in Europe: Concepts and Histories*, ed. Kari Palonen, Tuija Pulkkinen, and José M. Rosales (Farnham: Routledge, 2009), pp. 235–50; Wiesner, *Inventing the EU as a Democratic Polity: Concepts, Actors and Controversies* (London: Macmillan, 2019).

9. T.H. Marshall, *Citizenship and Social Class and Other Essays* (Cambridge: CUP, 1950), pp. 28–29; Charles Tilly, "Reflections on the History of European State-Making" in *The Formation of National States in Western Europe*, ed. Charles Tilly (Princeton, NJ: Princeton University Press, 1975), p. 32.

10. Marshall, *Citizenship and Social Class*.

11. Wiesner, *Bürgerschaft und Demokratie*; Wiesner, "Women's Partial Citizenship."

12. Seyla Benhabib (ed.), *Democracy and Difference: Contesting the Boundaries of the Political* (Princeton, NJ: Princeton

University Press, 1996); Jürgen Habermas, *The Inclusion of the Other*, ed. Ciaran P. Cronin and Pablo De Greiff (Cambridge MA: The MIT Press, 1998); Charles Taylor, *Multiculturalism and the Politics of Recognition* (Princeton, NJ: Princeton University Press, 1992); Iris Marion Young, *Justice and the Politics of Difference* (Princeton, NJ: Princeton University Press, 1990).

13. Armin Schäfer, Robert Vehrkamp, and Jérémie Felix Gagné, *Prekäre Wahlen. Milieus und soziale Selektivität der Wahlbeteiligung bei der Bundestagswahl 2013*, unpublished manuscript, http://www.wahlbeteiligung2013.de/fileadmin/Inhalte/Studien/Wahlbeteiligung-2013-Studie.pdf, (accessed November 9, 2021).

14. Claudia Wiesner, *Multi-Level-Governance und lokale Demokratie: Politikinnovationen im Vergleich* (Wiesbaden: Springer, 2018).

15. Marshall, *Citizenship and Social Class*, p. 77.

16. Marshall, *Citizenship and Social Class*, pp. 40, 62, 75.

17. This is also emphasized by Marshall.

CHAPTER 15

FREEDOM AND TAXES

RUDOLF MELLINGHOFF

I. INTRODUCTION

Anyone enquiring how much freedom we must forgo to be free will find tax to be a subject that is dominated by this relationship of tension. The tax state is characterized by the requirement to finance the state through taxes, while leaving labor and capital, the factors of production, in private hands. Taxes are therefore generally regarded as a justified encroachment on freedom, with civil liberties then determining the extent to which the state is allowed to have access to its citizens' private financial resources. Fyodor Dostoevsky pointed out early on that "money is freedom in the form of coins."[1] The financial means available to the individual form the basis of their personal freedom. Tax burdens impinge upon the civil liberties of citizens, who in turn set limits to the taxation imposed by the state.

II. THE TAX STATE

In order to be able to exercise its state powers effectively, the state needs financial resources. As early as the 16th century, the theoretician of the state Jean Bodin wrote that finances were the "nerves of the commonwealth."[2] Up until the 18th century, the state was mainly financed by the income the nobility extracted from their estates. It was not until the 19th century that the modern state developed into a tax state. At the end of the 19th century, the German economist Lorenz von Stein was able to state that taxes "have so outclassed all other sources of public revenue as to make them seem almost insignificant."[3] It was only in the 20th century, however, that the concept of the tax state as a state that is essentially financed by taxes was developed and given a theoretical basis.

III. THE TAX STATE AND THE FREE MARKET ECONOMY

The tax state is a basic condition of a free market economy. In order to generate income, it forgoes any economic activity of its own and leaves the production factors of labor and capital in private hands. This contrasts with socialist forms of government, which are financed by contributions from state and public services, and with state capitalism, which requires state ownership of the key industries. The tax state recognizes freedom of profession and ownership and for its part acquires the freedom through tax contributions to manage income and expenditure.[4] A prerequisite for the tax state is a market economy in which capital and labor remain basically in private hands and the state limits itself to participating in the economic success of the private sector.

The state's participation in the economic success of the individual is the price of freedom.[5] By leaving capital and labor basically in private hands and participating in the result of this work only through taxes, the state secures the foundations of freedom, economic freedom in particular. The tax state respects freedom and relies on the manufacturing economy making enough profit on its own terms that sufficient funds are available to fulfil the functions of the state. The tax state thus turns out to be better able to protect freedom than any other form of public finance.[6]

Although the state in a social market economy regulates the conditions under which the private sector engages in business, thus restricting economic freedoms, the tax state presupposes a fundamental separation of state and business. In such a form of government, both the state and the economy can pursue their own rationales.[7] While the state is primarily committed to the common good and social justice, for the economy the pursuit of profit is paramount. It is essential for a company to make a profit in the long term because this is the only way to safeguard its livelihood. This focus on profit means that a corresponding economic system is considerably more efficient than a socialist state that operates on its own behalf.

On the other hand, it is up to the state to establish the economic conditions through which the public interest and the common good can be asserted. For example, the state limits economic freedoms by regulating working conditions, by establishing guidelines for the protection of public safety and order, and by setting up rules concerning sustainability and climate protection. Such conditions are essential for the future viability of our society and for focusing on the common good. However, since the state is dependent on the economic success of companies, it also has an interest in ensuring that the performance of the economy overall is not impaired by its regulations. This guarantees a core of free economic activity, which is a prerequisite for the functioning of the tax state. At the same time, the state can set the conditions that work towards the common good in an appropriate manner.

Finally, the social dimension of the tax state provides opportunities for freedom and leads to the equalization of wealth disparities.[8] Taxation based on ability to pay takes economic differences into account and makes subsistence-level income tax-exempt. At the same time, tax provides the state with the financial resources to grant welfare state benefits based on need. Socially oriented taxation enables the state to take into account the distribution of income and wealth, level economic differences, and guarantee political freedoms. Moris Lehner expressed this connection in a striking way when he wrote that the welfare state and the tax state are linked through the state's joint responsibility for the freedom of its citizens, and that they fulfil this responsibility in mutual dependency.[9]

IV. THE TAX STATE AS THE DEMOCRATIC CONSTITUTIONAL STATE'S FORM OF GOVERNMENT

The tax state is the form of public finance that is appropriate to democracy. With the emergence of democracy, public finance through taxes came to dominate. The principle that no taxation should be possible without elected political representation ("no taxation without representation") forms the core of democratic decision-making. Parliament's right to set a budget is almost inconceivable without taxes.

In a democracy, parliament's decision as to which tasks money should be spent on must be made independently of where the funds come from. The principle of universality guarantees freedom of political action by means of the option of establishing priorities for expenditure on a case-by-case basis, without being bound by the purpose of taxation. In a democratic constitutional state, the financing of government tasks cannot be carried out on the principle of quid pro quo, so that taxes alone remain a suitable financing mechanism.[10]

V. TAXATION AND CIVIL LIBERTIES

If the principle of the tax state guarantees the general encroachment on freedom through the imposition of taxation as a necessary prerequisite for a functioning democratic constitutional state, at the same time limits are required to protect the individual's civil liberties. The principle of equal treatment is indeed considered to be the Magna Carta of tax law.[11] As long as other taxpayers with comparable ability to pay have to bear the same tax burden, the level of this burden cannot be challenged under equality law. As it is structured in a relative and open way, the principle of equal treatment does not specify a scope of protection that can be determined absolutely, and from which an upper limit for the burden of the state's access to taxes could be derived independently of a peer group.[12] Only constitutional guarantees of freedom offer protection against excessive taxation.

In this area, the limits of taxation as determined by civil liberties also answer the question of how much freedom we must forgo to be free. In Germany, no precise numerical taxation limits can be inferred from the civil liberties specified by the Basic Law; however, they provide a framework for taxation that is based on freedom. The less constitutional lawyers are concerned that a tax system is tending towards a lack of moderation or inadmissible restrictions on freedom, the more the system is based on freedom.

VI. THE TAX STATE AND FREEDOM

The principle of the tax state and tax limits based on freedom characterize the financing of the state based on civil liberties. They form the foundations of a free, democratic constitutional state which, on the one hand, guarantees social security and freedom through state services and, at the same time, respects the free system of labor and capital as well as property remaining in the hands of private individuals, and ensures the freedom of the citizen by imposing constitutional limits on the state's access to taxes.

State access to privately generated financial resources is necessary in order to carry out government tasks and thus to guarantee the care, protection, and security of the individual. The limitations placed on freedom by taxation are therefore a necessary prerequisite for freedom in terms of independence, dignity, and security, the kind of freedom that the social and democratic constitutional state wants to guarantee. On the other hand, constitutional limits are needed, as the financing of government tasks in itself knows no limits. Therefore, the civil liberties of taxpayers complement the free and democratic tax state and ensure moderate taxation. The principle of the tax state and the civil liberties of citizens together lead to taxation that does justice to freedom.

Notes

1. Fyodor Dostoevsky, *The House of the Dead*, trans. David McDuff (Harmondsworth: Penguin, 1985), p. 40. The Federal Constitutional Court makes this reference in connection with Art. 14 GG (BVerfG of March 31, 1998 – 2 BvR 1877/97 –, BVerfGE 97, 350, note 88).

2. Jean Bodin, *The Six Books of the Commonwealth*, abr. and trans. M.J. Tooley (Oxford: Blackwell, 1955), p. 91.

3. Lorenz von Stein, "On Taxation" in Richard A. Musgrave and Alan T. Peacock (eds.), *Classics in the Theory of Public Finance* (London/New York: Macmillan/St Martin's Press, 1967), p. 28. For more in the history of this development, see Klaus Vogel, "Der Finanz- und Steuerstaat" in *Handbuch des Staatsrechts* [*HStR*] II, ed. Josef Isensee and Paul Kirchhof, 3rd edn. (Heidelberg: C.F. Müller Verlag, 2004), § 30, note 55; Klaus Vogel and Christian Waldhoff in Wolfgang Kahl, Christian Waldhoff, and Christian Walter, *Bonner Kommentar zum Grundgesetz*, Preliminary Remarks on Art. 104A–115, note 327 ff.

4. Josef Isensee, "Staatsvermögen" in *Handbuch des Staatsrechts* [*HStR*] V, ed. Josef Isensee and Paul Kirchhof, 3rd edn., (Heidelberg: C.F. Müller Verlag, 2007), § 122, note 70.

5. Michael Rodi, "Der Steuerstaat" in *Territorialität und Personalität. Festschrift für Moris Lehner* (Cologne: De Gruyter, 2019), p. 377 (380) with reference to Stefan Grunow, *Die verfassungsrechtliche Rechtfertigung der Steuerlast und der Steuererhebung* (Baden-Baden: Nomos Verlag, 2018), pp. 76 ff.; cf. also Paul Kirchhof, "Die Steuer ist der Preis der Freiheit, Die Steuern" in *Handbuch des Staatsrechts [HStR]* V ³2007, § 118, note 2.

6. Rodi, "Der Steuerstaat."

7. For more on this and the following, see Vogel, "Der Finanz- und Steuerstaat," § 30, note 59 ff.

8. For more on this, see Rodi, "Der Steuerstaat," pp. 382 f.

9. Moris Lehner, *Einkommensteuerrecht und Sozialhilferecht* (Tübingen: Mohr Siebeck, 1993), p. 360.

10. Rodi, "Der Steuerstaat," p. 379.

11. Cf. Roman Herzog, "Steuer- und Finanzpolitik im geeinten Deutschland. Die Sicht des Bundesverfassungsgerichts" in *Steuer und Finanzpolitik im geeinten Deutschland und Europa, Deutscher Steuerzahler Kongress*, ed. Bund der Steuerzahler (Wiesbaden, 1991), p. 10 (11).

12. Joachim Englisch, *Steuer und Wirtschaft [StuW]*, 2003, p. 237 (237).

CHAPTER 16

FREEDOM OUT OF THE PASSION FOR ORDER: A MINIMALLY INVASIVE AUTOPSY OF LIBERALISM

BAZON BROCK

Seasoned by routine and strengthened by disappointment, those who want to justify a short interim report on their activities in the public arena take but a few small steps, while attributing great importance to them nonetheless. So when experienced professionals justify themselves by referring not to what they know but to what they don't know, this seems to be just such a small step.

Novices are motivated by the prospect of acquiring knowledge to set them apart from others; experienced individuals emphasize where they are in agreement with others, that is in knowing as little as they do. What they have in common is the experience that every gain in knowledge only makes it all the more clear what an individual doesn't or doesn't yet know about dealing with a problematic situation. But as soon as the individual thinks they are getting closer to overcoming the "not yet," they lose their initial optimism (compare the common experience of finding it impossible to reach the horizon). But beware: this is not the admission of the much-lauded *ignorabimus*.[1] On the one hand, since the time of Socrates the most productive form of knowledge has been characterized as knowing that one knows nothing; and on the other hand, all humanity is based on understanding that they too cannot progress further than people always have. The premise of this is of course the assumption that people are equal.

Whichever way you look at it, people are not equal because of their genetic make-up, social background, or educational career. By contrast, the inalienable assertion of equality can actually be justified and fulfilled in every respect, if we remember that all people—whether road sweepers or professors—are totally equal in what they don't know, can't do, and don't have. The extent of what we don't know, as all those who know say, is unimaginably greater than what people do know, whether it's kept in books, buildings, or on computer servers. Even attempts at individual self-aggrandizement through spiritual exercises or metaphysical speculations don't help, although they offer consolation to some poor souls in the face of their endless pursuit of knowledge.

Now the aforementioned equality of people in the face of the imposition of not-knowing provides the basis for constructing sense and contexts of meaning, insofar as sense emerges by linking various meanings together. Meaning arises by making distinctions according to criteria.

It is extremely unfortunate when, as is commonplace today, the inequality of people is inferred from the inequality of criteria for making distinctions. Of course, rabbit breeders, art historians, automobile manufacturers, or bakers each follow specific and very different criteria for making distinctions in order to give meaning to what they do. But in establishing the sense of their actions by linking meanings, they all fulfil what it means to prove oneself to be a human being among other human beings in an equally exemplary way.

In this context, freedom essentially means freedom of choice and access to the various social systems of creating meanings. For example, in order to be able to choose a profession, you have to know the criteria for creating sense in the activities specific to that profession, otherwise you are just left with the freedom to do nothing. However, as experience shows, this is always rapidly exhausted (nothing is harder to bear than several days without work). Freedom from the obligation to make distinctions ends up in a loss of focus created by whim. In principle, freedom from the obligation to act meaningfully cannot exist. If you don't want to adopt the criteria of bakers, art historians, or automobile manufacturers, you have to create your own criteria as artists do, for example. However, this is much more demanding and riskier than taking advantage of the systems of creating sense that have been provided and often tried and tested by society, i.e., professions in the world of work.

In order to avoid the predictable conflicts between effective personal criteria for creating sense by individuals and the criteria provided by society, people have always seen their communities as guarantors of the systems that have harmonized the relationship between religious or party-political beliefs, career choice, and social obligations. Only such systems enable the kind of freedom that goes beyond "might is right". The latter comes into its own precisely because all sense in life is imposed only by the dictates of just a few rigid criteria in making distinctions. But once again we should beware: even a formally democratic society can exercise totalitarian power if it recognizes as economic entities only those individuals who agree to make a profit through their activities. But who would trust a doctor, psychologist, or social worker who has to accept that the state-approved success of their work lies in making a profit by providing care?

This explains the reference to the basic principle of our systems of order: the binding systems must not cancel each other out, because then members of the community lose all confidence in the systems that generate sense. For example, tax law should not be set up in such a way that even specialist tax consultants find it almost impossible to do justice to it, while at the same time forcing every taxpayer, on pain of prosecution, to observe all the regulations and submit a complete tax return. Such instances where the systems of social coherence are corroded do not increase freedom of action, as neo-liberals like to claim, but rather destroy it. For example, at least since the totalitarianism of the National Socialist regime we have known that destroying freedom does not enhance the validity of systems but only the whims of those in power. All of today's totalitarian regimes of Chinese,

Russian, Turkish, or other origin do not lead to the triumph of the power of their rigid systems but to the arbitrariness of any conveniently justifiable claims to power that can no longer be challenged, for example by reference to existing laws. Legal systems are inherently the first targets of the whims of the powerful.

Those who advance a choice between order or freedom destroy both and are not in any way establishing a higher law, whether nationalist or divine.

Note

1. *Ignoramus et ignorabimus* ("we do not know and will not know") is a phrase coined by physiologist Emil Heinrich Du Bois-Reymond. It has become famous as expressing skepticism of the natural sciences' claims to be able to explain everything. https://en.wikipedia.org/wiki/Ignoramus_et_ignorabimus (accessed February 3, 2022).

CHAPTER 17

FREEDOM, RHYTHMS, AND RESTRICTION

HANS ULRICH OBRIST AND MARTHA JUNGWIRTH IN CONVERSATION

During the CONVOCO! Forum on July 31, 2021, in Salzburg, Hans Ulrich Obrist talked to the artist Martha Jungwirth about art and freedom. Martha Jungwirth's extraordinary practice spans over six decades, and uses a visual language that is both figurative and abstract. She experiments with new ideas as well as pursuing a consistent mark-making process, as is the case with her most recent series, *Corona Diaries*. Jungwirth's work has always been an exploration of the personal, as well as an engagement with the history of art, Greek mythology, poetry, and the environment. Obrist sat down with Martha Jungwirth to discuss these themes, as well as what freedom means in the 21st century.

Hans Ulrich Obrist: It's a great pleasure for me to welcome Martha Jungwirth to the CONVOCO! Forum. When Corinne Flick called me and told me about the topic "How much freedom must we forgo to be free?" I went first to my mentor Édouard Glissant, the great philosopher and thinker from Martinique who died a few years ago, to see what he had to say on the subject. He says: "L'identité c'est la participation à l'autre." Identity means participation with the other. "Pour participer à l'autre il faut être libre." To participate with the other you have to be free. He defines freedom as being available to approach others in order to live together. It then occurred to me that in 1997 with curator Hou Hanru I organized the 100th anniversary exhibition *Cities on the Move* at the Vienna Secession. There, every day, we were confronted with Ludwig Hevesi's motto, which was written on the facade of the Secession Building in 1897 and remains there today: "Der Zeit ihre Kunst, der Kunst ihre Freiheit," "To the age its art, to art its freedom." Then I visited Martha Jungwirth's studio on the suggestion of the painter Albert Oehlen. He told me that Martha Jungwirth's work was about free painting. It's never about a reductive program, about an *a priori*, rather the pictures invent themselves while she's painting and have done so for over six decades. Martha Jungwirth has discovered a unique language between figuration and abstraction, always observing the space and the landscape around her. We're going to talk about that. Of course, over the past few years there have been restrictions. Among other things, it has not really been possible to visit museums over the last 18 months.[1] That has changed the way we work. And as always, Martha Jungwirth's art is seismographic. It's about rhythms, it's about freedom, it's about restriction. We're so happy that she is here with us today. I promised not to talk too much about the past but rather about the present. So I'll ask just one question about the past. Once in the 1990s I was in Antoni Tàpies' studio, and he talked about the freedom of Informalism in the postwar 1950s. You too once told me that this was important for you, that Informalism and Abstract Expressionism suited your nature and your way of thinking. Can you tell us something about that?

Martha Jungwirth: When I was studying in Vienna, the famous Galerie nächst St Stephan was run by Monseigneur Mauer, and it was there that I met four important Austrian painters for the first time: Josef

Mikl, Arnulf Rainer, Wolfgang Hollegha, and Markus Prachensky. I was a new student and really didn't have a clue. But when I saw these pictures, I thought: "Aha, this is a possibility. This is my path." I don't want to imitate reality. I start with nature, but I want to do something equivalent, something different. Nature is just an excuse, a stimulus, if you will.

HUO: I was in your studio for the first time—your studio really is a world unto itself—when you were working on the big picture, which went on to decorate the fire curtain at the Vienna Opera for twelve months. When I entered the studio I saw a Trojan Horse and that was your idea from the start. Can you tell us more about this big picture and your work at the Opera?

MJ: I've always engaged with Greek mythology, and it occurred to me that in opera too things emerge, whether for good or evil. And so, I thought that this mythological animal, which represents so much, would actually be an interesting motif. And that's what happened. My way of working is intended to be a free movement, something associative. And of course, there are also images and models in art history that have stuck in my mind, for example Lovis Corinth's *The Trojan Horse*. That's why I was interested in this subject.

HUO: As is so often the case in your work, there was an element of restriction, and in this case it was the color red. When I was in your studio, I could see only red pictures.

MJ: Yes, red—it has a certain something. I practically have to force myself to use other colors. There are all kinds of shades, from the lightest, most delicate flesh tones to the darkest, most fetid blood-red. The color is also mythologically freighted and embedded in practice. I'm drawn to working with this color palette.

HUO: Let's go back to your method. In many of your pictures over the decades there has always been a constellation of blotches. It's not fixed, but it is, as you said, fluid—it's open.

MJ: Yes, my background is actually watercolor, where you have freedom, so to speak. Fixed, dry watercolors are the most hideous. For me, the color has to flow, it has to move freely, and this creates new blotches. And then in my second phase I came to oil painting. In this medium you can create wonderfully thin, transparent, superimposed, and layered effects or lumps, blobs, and clusters. I was interested in this as a different medium. What can I do with this solid paint?

HUO: Gustav Metzger, the legendary artist who has always dealt with climate issues, once said: "We have to restrict freedom in order to address the issue of the climate." You've painted many animals, inspired by apocalyptic images from Australia.

MJ: Yes, I found it so horrific, these forest fires and the millions of animals that perished. And all this killing and decimating of different species carries on. This topic, which used to affect me less, has now become very interesting for me. Then I started painting animals. In addition, my style of painting with oils was somehow heavy in the past, the blotches more layered on top of each other. But after this first half of the pandemic, I was kind of exhausted. I noticed how people became cut off from everything. You can't go to a museum, which is very important to me because I am interested in what other painters do. You can always learn from other artists. These realities of other artists create an interplay that interests me very much. But it just wasn't allowed, and you're left to your own devices in the studio. Then I suddenly noticed how everything was becoming less and less, how everything was actually being reduced to its skeleton form.

And then my subject matter was animals. Death was practically in the air. And I have to say that the pandemic helped me a lot. I read the *Frankfurter Allgemeine* every morning and there were interesting pieces, for example a photo of Tutankhamun's tomb. This took me back to my own past, because I once spent a week in Cairo, visited the pyramids, and then I went to Saqqara with my husband. Suddenly this photo brought layers of memory to life, so to speak, and got me interested in this topic, otherwise I wouldn't have thought about it at all. So I reactivated things that I came across by chance and with which I have a relationship, and turned them into painting.

HUO: There was another article at that time when you couldn't leave the house and you were just getting newspaper deliveries. It was an article on Alice Oswald, and it was particularly significant. It's related to this new cycle that you have created. It's about *The Iliad* and *The Odyssey*.

MJ: There was a book review in the *Frankfurter Allgemeine* about an English poet named Alice Oswald, in which she wrote that she had found *The Iliad* so inspiring. But her fantastic poetry is somehow absurd. Her main subject is not the classical heroes, rather she writes about the reality of being foot soldiers and all the misery that happened over the course of this war using very modern and very sensitive, wonderful language. And that fascinated me. Maybe I can read you a brief extract:

> Also ADRESTUS and AMPHIUS
>
> Everyone knew they were going to die
>
> They were the sons of Merops the prophet
>
> He begged them to stay at home but they couldn't listen
>
> Their own ghosts were calling them to Troy
>
> Immaculate in clean linen
>
> They set out together but Death
>
> Was already walking to meet them[2]

The way she describes all this killing is what inspired my work. It's a wonderful book. I can't recommend it too highly.

HUO: And this book, *Memorial. An Excavation of the Iliad*, also led to the title of your cycle, which will be shown in Paris in September and October 2021. When we had coffee today, you mentioned something very interesting: you said that during these restrictions it was about not being able to escape yourself. Can you explain that?

MJ: Well, in such circumstances you are also subject to your own constraints, of course. That's when you realize how many you've got. So with my work I tried to address my fears, my constraints, and everything I had that was, so to speak, cut off. I thought that at this time, when you can't and don't want to enjoy any kind of pleasure, I have to do something at least. I have to use the time to make something happen.

HUO: Your *Corona Diaries* were created during lockdown. They are blotches on cardboard. You coined this famous phrase: "A blotch is a blotch is a blotch." And you once told me that there are "intelligent" blotches, but also "stupid" blotches.

MJ: Yes, you can see that in other painters' work too. How interesting is a constellation of blotches? How much is my own invention? How can I change that? An important moment in my work is coincidence, that is bringing about coincidence. You have an idea, but this idea sometimes solidifies and then something happens in the painting process that you don't expect. You have to grasp the chance occurrence, so to speak, and use it as a further element. You have to observe, step back, and the best thing is to stop thinking completely and just paint. I have a weakness for old pieces of cardboard with blotches on them. If it's not pure white, I actually prefer it. Sometimes I have a horror of white, because I have to put the first blotch on it, and it can be good or bad. But when the blotch is already there in some way, you're less anxious. I'm always working on different things at the same time in order to stay in the flow. If you somehow feel that you are becoming permeable and it's all going in, then of course that is what you are striving for. Sometimes it stalls and then I do small things in between on tatty bits of cardboard—it's very practical, because there is still paint on the brush—but you're not controlling so much. This is how you can reintroduce an uncontrolled element so that it doesn't get boring. And those were my so-called *Corona Diaries*, something immediate, not "now I'm going to do a big picture." A large picture is exhausting, but you can move easily between smaller ones. And that has an effect in return. Something unconscious or uncomplicated can be used again for other things. That's my method.

HUO: You once told me that it's often an adventure, an adventure in seeing. When you paint you're creating seismographic records, states of excitement. This idea of the adventure in seeing is interesting. Oskar Kokoschka founded the School of Seeing here in Salzburg. You also spoke of the freedom of seeing. Can you tell us something more about that?

MJ: Your gaze feels its way. You have to work as if straddling between your hand and eye somehow, otherwise it looks too well-behaved and controlled and I don't want that. I want to put something on canvas or on paper that is open-ended so that everyone who looks at it—including myself—can make something new from it. So nothing is fixed, nothing controlled. It should stay interesting, able to be looked at again with new eyes. That's what I'm interested in.

HUO: There's this state of excitement, and then at some point you stop. When is a painting finished?

MJ: Sometimes you know that immediately. You can't do anything more, otherwise it'll be ruined. Sometimes you don't know right away, but think to yourself: "I could add another blotch now." But I'd prefer to be careful, put it aside, and do something new, either something small or something else big. After two or three weeks you can face the old things completely freely. So either it will be ruined or it will become something. Sometimes it doesn't work out and you have to throw it away, but sometimes with just a few more blotches it can turn out very well.

HUO: If you look at the different decades of your work, there are breaks and continuities. You once said that one can identify basic models that you have used over the decades—basic models that actually return again and again in all phases of your work, albeit with various modifications. Can you tell us more about that?

MJ: Yes, I looked at that. I certainly have a basic pattern of blotches and lines. Certain colors appear again and again, certain movements too. Of course you have to try to change the movement, the repertoire of gestures, and I try to do that again and again. The basic attitude or my view of how I perceive the world is inscribed within me, but it always has to be modified. And that also changes because you yourself are developing, because you perceive things differently. For example, other artists whom you value or valued less in the past are suddenly seen differently. This is also an interesting dialogue with art history.

HUO: That's true too—it's a permanent dialogue with art history through regular museum visits.

MJ: Yes, I am very interested in other artists' other reality, because it's a world that is just wonderful. If you go to a great exhibition, you come out a different person. It makes tiny tweaks to your own development.

HUO: Gerhard Richter once said to me "Art is the highest form of hope." And when I quoted that today, you said that for you art is a gateway to freedom.

MJ: Reality is just reality—you have to submit to certain things. But when you are alone with yourself, with the paints, the support, your own hands, and the brushes, that's a wonderful thing. And sometimes something really good comes out of it.

HUO: Robert Louis Stevenson once said that art is like children playing. It's about play, but it also has the seriousness of children playing. You once said, "I am my own child"—an interesting phrase. Can you explain that to us?

MJ: How can I explain that? It's playfulness and somehow irresponsibility—I'm responsible only to myself and no one else. Nobody can interfere with what I do; I'm my own boss, and that's something wonderful. When you're a child, you own the whole world and you can do what you want. And I can do whatever I want on the support and with the paints.

HUO: I have one final question that I ask in all interviews. Do you have an unrealized project?

MJ: Just to keep on working.

Notes

1. This was because of the COVID-19 pandemic.
2. Alice Oswald, *Memorial: An Excavation of The Iliad* (London: Faber, 2011).

CHAPTER 18

FREEDOM IN THE ANTHROPOCENE

PHILIPP PATTBERG

"Making peace with nature is the defining task of the 21st century."

António Guterres,
United Nations Secretary-General[1]

"Freedom in the commons brings ruin to all."[2] This is the enduring insight of an otherwise questionable paper by biologist Garrett Hardin published in 1968. "Commons" is referred to as the resources (both cultural and natural) accessible to all members of a society and hence not privately owned. The atmosphere can be considered such a common. By adding greenhouse gases to the atmosphere, humankind (to largely different degrees) contributes to climate change and its associated direct impacts such as sea-level rise and increased frequency of extreme weather events (including flooding and drought), as well as to indirect impacts such as food scarcity, migration, and biodiversity loss. What scientists are increasingly worried about are so-called tipping points, abrupt changes in previously stable systems that lead to new equilibria with often disastrous consequences. For example, recent scientific data makes it likely that the Antarctic Thwaites Glacier, the widest glacier on the planet, will have shed large parts of its shelf within the next five years, contributing to further accelerated melting and consequent sea-level rise.[3]

To mitigate climate change at around 1.5 degrees of warming compared to pre-industrial averages, current emissions must drastically decline to zero, leaving no more than 7.5 years before the global carbon budget will be exhausted.[4] Can we avert climate breakdown without limiting our political and individual freedoms, or does addressing the climate challenge require giving up freedom? In this essay, I argue that we don't need to give up freedom to fight climate change if we act quickly, but we risk our freedom if we act too slowly or not at all. What we need to give up instead of our freedom is our taken-for-granted privileges.

I will proceed as follows. Section I will review the relationship between freedom, progress, and unsustainability. Section II outlines three areas of transition that will keep the 1.5-degree goal of the Paris Agreement alive. Section III will in turn discuss the necessary scope conditions for transformative change, in particular what we can learn from the global COVID-19 pandemic for balancing radical mitigation with personal and political freedom.

I. FREEDOM IN THE HOLOCENE

Human civilization and, in an indirect way, freedom and political liberties too are a result of the stable climatic conditions of the Holocene. Over the last 11,000 years, our planetary climate system has displayed an extraordinary stability, enabling *Homo sapiens* to invent agriculture, religion, and politics. Climate change is now threatening this Holocene state. To be more precise, human activities, many related to unconstrained freedom, have pushed the Earth's system into a new state, the Anthropocene.

The relationship between liberal freedom and sustainability is nuanced, and is impossible to review in such a short essay. Freedom to act without ideological constraints and based only on reason allows us to choose sustainable alternatives over non-sustainable ones. On the other hand, unconstrained freedom, for example in the form of contemporary hyperconsumerism, will lead to system breakdown. Within a limited biophysical system, freedom has its limits, too. Freedom as the product of the Enlightenment is ideologically bound to the process of ever-greater individualization and the subsequent nature–culture dichotomy, which in turn enables the plundering of the planet. In other words, freedom has co-created the conditions for environmental breakdown. To protect ourselves from civilizational breakdown, we need to rethink what freedom can be: not maximized individual choices but connectedness to the greater whole.

To secure a livable future and safeguard our freedoms, we need to limit our destructive behavior in the present. We need to use our freedom to refrain from activities that jeopardize our freedom in the future. What might be perceived as freedom is often just what we are used to—normalized and privileged behavior that has become institutionalized into bad habits. Driving a combustion-engine SUV or taking the plane on a long-distance vacation is not about freedom but about privilege.[5] Instead of a discourse about giving up certain material assets we should discuss changing unsustainable habits into sustainable ones. What helps here is the concept of functional equivalence. As the saying goes, "I don't need a drill, but a hole in the wall." We seem to confuse the concrete manifestation of a manufactured desire (the biggest SUV, the newest smartphone) with the deeper need it should ideally serve. We don't need individual motorized transportation, but rather mobility; we don't need a new smartphone, but rather connectivity; we don't need a particular kind of energy, such as coal, gas, or nuclear, but rather warmth, light, and electricity. In short, we don't need to give up freedom as a political category. Freedom will not be impacted by the deeper societal transition towards sustainability, but our bad habits and privileges will.

II. KEEPING 1.5 DEGREES ALIVE

The recent global climate negotiations that took place in Glasgow (COP 26) in late 2021 have ended with a broadly accepted agreement, the Glasgow Climate Pact.[6] While not without shortcomings, the Glasgow Pact commits governments and non-state actors to more ambitious climate actions. In fact, a 1.5-degree world is still possible with the given technology and if actors realize their commitments. Implementing these commitments, for example the phase-down of coal and harmful fossil fuel subsidies, will require drastic, fast, and costly actions, but will not affect our freedoms. However, delaying drastic action will impact freedom in the future. Different scenarios are plausible. In the first scenario, action is delayed but eventually happens (albeit very late). As a result, drastic emergency measures must be taken, impacting our political and personal freedoms. In the second scenario, we do not act at all but follow the business-as-usual path, leading up to around 4 to 6 degrees of warming by the end of this century. Societies will face climate breakdown and the associated disruptions, including violent conflict, starvation, and mass migration. Also, a climate-constrained future will imply that there are fewer choices (individual freedom), for example, in terms of where to live or what profession to pursue. In the third scenario, we act quickly and decisively and thereby maintain freedoms but give up privileges and habits.

Meeting the 1.5-degree target is still within the range of feasible scenarios. What must happen? There are three broad and deep transitions that must happen quickly and in parallel but are feasible given our current technological and political constellations. First, our energy system has to transition to a renewable and primarily electricity-based system (with some bridging and additional technologies such as Green Hydrogen). In addition to the broad electrification of various sectors, including transportation and heating and the fast scaling-up of renewables in final energy consumption,[7] reducing energy consumption by reconsidering practices and technologies will be key.

The second transition concerns our current use of space, both on land and in the ocean. The current expansionist regime of using ever more space for human purposes has to quickly change to one in which we protect nature and allow sufficient room for processes of rewilding. As of 2020, only 17 percent of land environments are protected, while experts call for global protection levels of 30 to 50 percent.[8]

The third important transition concerns our food system. Total greenhouse gas emissions from the food system, including supply-chain activities, amounted to 34 percent of global emissions in 2015.[9] In addition to the climate impact of our food system, it not only drives land-use change and thereby directly threatens biodiversity, but it also contributes to human health problems[10] and the immense suffering of other sentient beings.[11] Science is clear in advising a predominantly plant-based diet and subsequent localized food system.

These three transitions conversely imply that we must end the three broad activities that have become habits: extracting fossil fuels, destroying nature, and exploiting animals for human consumption. While each of these constitutes a deep-seated habit, leaving them behind and transitioning to a more sustainable pattern will not mean a loss of freedom but rather a gain. We might give up individualized combustion-based mobility, but gain public health, livable space, and urban biodiversity, to name a few. For these transitions to work out, some more fundamental conditions need to be in place. We will discuss these in the next section.

III. TOWARDS TRANSFORMATIVE CHANGE

As we are slowly navigating out of the global COVID-19 pandemic, we realize that this global health crisis and climate change are intricately linked. Not only does climate change and the underlying patterns of nature destruction increase the likelihood of zoonotic diseases,[12] our responses to the COVID-19 pandemic, in particular decisions how we will build back, have a major impact on climate change. In the words of United Nations Secretary-General António

Guterres: "We cannot go back to the old normal of inequality, injustice, and heedless dominion over the Earth. Instead, we must step towards a safer, more sustainable, and equitable path. The door is open; the solutions are there."[13] The next sections outline the necessary conditions for transformative change, change that is not just symbolic but touches upon the deeper layers of our unsustainability. I am particularly interested in what lessons we can learn from the pandemic on how to achieve transformative change without jeopardizing our freedom.

The first condition for achieving transformative change is to develop a narrative that clearly outlines the ultimate goal and necessary steps towards that goal (in our concrete case, the goal of sustainability and making peace with nature), while at the same time incorporating different viewpoints and perspectives. What rapidly became apparent in the COVID-19 pandemic was that simply justifying concrete measures (such as wearing masks) did not create sufficient support for the overall goal to fight the virus, because the ultimate goal was insufficiently outlined in a way that would incorporate various worldviews and legitimate perspectives. A similar observation can be made in the case of climate change. While concrete measures such as electric mobility or reducing personal air miles are discussed, we lack a broader societal debate about how we envisage the world in 2050 (when global emissions are zero) and what steps can guide us there, beyond the technical aspects of timelines and gigatonnes. For example, will 2050 be a world of the privileged few who control carbon-free technologies and extort huge profits from these, or rather a world where not only emissions per capita are similar, but also lifestyles, life-expectancies, and chances? Clearly outlining alternative zero-emission futures with the help of broader meta-narratives will not only help to mobilize support, but also clarify the necessary in-between steps.

The second condition for transformative change is the existence of a "reasonable majority." We have seen in the recent pandemic that a small but vocal part of society has decided to actively sabotage attempts to address complex challenges such as a global pandemic or climate change based on self-serving and self-sustaining ideologies. While COVID-19 and climate are not comparable in all their aspects when it comes to vocal minorities,[14] the lesson to be learned here is that these vocal minorities gain power only due to the sustained media and political attention they receive, and not because of their representative or intellectual power. However, while the majority of the population is often silent, it is out there and supports necessary measures, whether climate- or COVID-19-related.[15] This reasonable majority deserves support.

The third condition for transformative change is the realization that climate change calls for solidarity and justice. Again, the COVID-19 pandemic can serve as an important lesson. It is not surprising that the primary focus of debate is on domestic challenges and measures. However, both COVID-19 and climate change are essentially global public good problems. To achieve global health (in this concrete case the end of the COVID-19 pandemic), all countries need to achieve sufficient levels of vaccination and an adequate supply of public health services. This is a question of international solidarity and justice. The same is true for climate change. To successfully address this global challenge, we need solidarity with those countries that are most vulnerable and have contributed least to the problem. Climate change action is also deeply connected to discussions about fairness and justice. Embedded in the 1992 United Nations Framework Convention on Climate Change is the important principle of Common but Differentiated Responsibility that calls on rich developed countries to take on special responsibility and action, acknowledging not only their historic responsibilities but also their financial and technical abilities. While it is certainly crucial to realize climate change mitigation and adaptation with careful consideration of our basic and personal freedoms, climate change cannot be averted without taking solidarity, responsibility, and justice into account. As a reminder: under the 2015 Paris Agreement, even vulnerable low-lying island nations have taken on climate mitigation commitments (in the form of so-called Nationally Determined Contributions), but the industrialized countries have so far failed to realize their promise to contribute 100 billion dollars annually to climate actions by poor countries.

To sum up, we can avert climate breakdown without giving up our conception of freedom. What we have to abandon instead is institutionalized bad habits and privileges that can be substituted with sustainable functional equivalents. To leave behind wasteful lifestyles and business cycles, fossil fuels and a murderous food regime, we need to ensure a big integrative meta-narrative, international solidarity and focus on the silent, reasonable majority. Under these conditions, freedom and a stable climate are not a contradiction.

Notes

1. United Nations, Secretary-General's address at Columbia University: "The State of the Planet", December 2, 2020, https://www.un.org/sg/en/content/sg/statement/2020-12-02/secretary-generals-address-columbia-university-the-state-of-the-planet-scroll-down-for-language-versions (accessed February 14, 2022).

2. See Garrett Hardin, "The Tragedy of the Commons" in *Science* 162, 1968, pp. 1243–1248.

3. "Giant cracks push imperilled Antarctic glacier closer to collapse" in *Nature*, December 14, 2021, https://www.nature.com/articles/d41586-021-03758-y (accessed January 11, 2022).

4. To stay below 1.5 degrees of warming compared to the pre-industrial average, the atmosphere can absorb (with a baseline of 2020) some additional 400 gigatonnes of carbon dioxide, leaving roughly 7.5 years from January 2022 until the exhaustion of the carbon budget, at current rates of emissions. Staying below 2 degrees would give us a time window of about 25 years from now. See Mercator Research Institute on Global Commons and Climate Change, "That's how fast the carbon clock is ticking", https://www.mcc-berlin.net/en/research/co2-budget.html (accessed January 11, 2022).

5. *Privilege*: "An advantage that only one person or group of people has, usually because of their position or because they are rich." *Cambridge Dictionary*, https://dictionary.cambridge.org/dictionary/english/privilege (accessed January 11, 2022).

6. See United Nations, "COP26: The Glasgow Climate Pact", https://ukcop26.org (accessed January 11, 2022).

7. In 2019, the share of renewables in total final energy consumption was 11.2 percent, with fossil fuels making

up 80.2 percent, a similar figure to 2009. See REN21, "Key Messages", https://www.ren21.net/gsr-2021/pages/keymessages/keymessages/ (accessed January 11, 2022).

8. For example, the late E.O. Wilson was a fervent advocate of protecting half the planet for the benefit of biodiversity and climate protection, see Edward O. Wilson, *Half-Earth: Our Planet's Fight for Life* (New York: Liveright, 2016).

9. M. Crippa et al., "Food Systems are responsible for a third of global anthropogenic GHG emissions" in *Nature Food* 2, 2021, pp. 198–209, https://www.nature.com/articles/s43016-021-00225-9 (accessed January 11, 2022).

10. Walter Willet et al., "Food in the Anthropocene: the EAT-Lancet Commission on healthy diets from sustainable food systems" in *The Lancet Commissions* 393, 2019, pp. 447–492, https://www.thelancet.com/journals/lancet/article/PIIS0140-6736(18)31788-4/fulltext (accessed January 11, 2022).

11. It is estimated that in the United States of America alone, approximately 55 billion animals, excluding fish and shellfish, were killed for human consumption in 2021.

12. Rory Gibb et al., "Ecosystem perspectives are needed to manage zoonotic risks in a changing climate" in *BMJ* 371, 2020, https://www.ncbi.nlm.nih.gov/pmc/articles/PMC7662085/ (accessed January 11, 2022).

13. United Nations, Secretary General's address at Columbia University: "The State of the Planet."

14. One important difference is that COVID-19 deniers and other critics of public health measures are supported by populist parties, while the climate-denier movement was and still is supported by mainstream business. For a broader discussion of the involvement of the fossil fuel industry in financing climate-denier campaigns, see Naomi Oreskes and Erik M. Conway, *Merchants of Doubt: How a Handful of*

Scientists Obscured the Truth on Issues from Tobacco Smoke to Global Warming (London: Bloomsbury, 2010).

15. For example, recent Eurobarometer data shows that 90 percent of Europeans agree with reducing greenhouse gases to make the European Union climate neutral by 2050; 93 percent believe that climate change is a serious problem. European Commission, "Citizen Support for Climate Action: 2021 Survey", https://ec.europa.eu/clima/citizens/citizen-support-climate-action_en (accessed January 11, 2022).

CONTRIBUTORS

Univ. Prof. em. Dr.sc. tc. hc. Bazon Brock, thinker at large and artist without portfolio, is Emeritus Professor of Aesthetics and Cultural Education at the Bergische Universität in Wuppertal, Germany. Other professorships include at Hamburg University of Fine Arts (1965–76) and the University of Applied Arts, Vienna (1977–80). In 1992 he was awarded an honorary doctorate at ETH (Swiss Federal Institute for Technology, Zürich) and in 2012 at the Hochschule für Gestaltung, Karlsruhe. Since 2014 he has been Honorary Professor for Prophecy at HBKsaar (Saar College of Fine Arts), Saarbrücken. In 2016 he was awarded the Von der Heydt Prize by the City of Wuppertal and in 2017 the Austrian Cross of Honour for Science and Art. He has developed the method of "Action Teaching," in which the seminar hall becomes a place of enactment, for oneself and others. Between 1968 and 1992, he led the documenta schools for visitors, which he founded in Kassel. From 2010 to 2013 he ran courses for "professional citizens" at the Karlsruhe University of Arts and Design. He has organized around 3,000 events and "action plays," e.g. *Lustmarsch durchs Theoriegelände* (2006, in eleven museums). He is a member of the Institut für theoretische Kunst, Universalpoesie und Prognostik, and Founder of the Amt für Arbeit an unlösbaren Problemen und Maßnahmen der hohen Hand, Berlin (www.denkerei-berlin.de).

Prof. Dr. Tim Crane is a Professor of Philosophy at Central European University (CEU), Vienna. Before coming to CEU he was Knightbridge Professor of Philosophy at the University of Cambridge and a Fellow of Peterhouse from 2009. Before that he taught at UCL for 19 years, and founded the Institute of Philosophy in the University of London as its first Director in 2005. He was educated at the Universities of Durham, York, and Cambridge, where he obtained his Ph.D. in 1989. Crane is the author of many articles on philosophy of mind and metaphysics, and of the following books: *The Mechanical Mind* (1995, 3rd edition 2016), *Elements of Mind* (2001), *The Objects of Thought* (2013), *Aspects of Psychologism* (2014), and *The Meaning of Belief: Religion* *from an Atheist's Point of View* (2017). He was the editor of the *Routledge Encyclopedia of Philosophy*, and the philosophy consultant editor for the TLS. His work has been translated into Arabic, Chinese, Croatian, French, German, Hungarian, Italian, Japanese, Korean, Persian, Polish, Portuguese, Romanian, Spanish, and Swedish. He is currently working on the nature of the unconscious and on the nature of belief.

Prof. Gabriel Felbermayr, Ph.D. is Director of the Austrian Institute of Economic Research (WIFO) and a Professor at the Vienna University of Economics and Business. After studying economics and trade at the University of Linz, he went to Florence to pursue his doctoral studies. From 2004 to 2005, he was an Associate Consultant with McKinsey & Co. in Vienna. From 2005 to 2008, he was Assistant Professor at the University of Tübingen. From 2009 to 2010, he held a Chair in International Economics at the University of Hohenheim (Stuttgart). From 2010 to 2019, he led the ifo Center for International Economics at the University of Munich, where he also served as Professor of International Economics. From 2019 to September 2021, he was President of Kiel Institute for the World Economy. At the same time, he held a Chair in Economics and Economic Policy at Kiel University (CAU).

Gabriel Felbermayr is a member of the Scientific Advisory Board of the Germany Federal Ministry of Economics and Energy, and the Chairman of the Statistics Council at Statistics Austria. He is Associate Editor at the *European Economic Review*. Gabriel Felbermayr's research focuses on issues of international trade theory and policy, labor market research, European economic integration, and current economic policy issues. He has published a large number of papers in international scholarly journals, policy briefs, and newspapers. His research has been recognized with various awards.

Dr. Corinne Michaela Flick studied both law and literature, taking American studies as her subsidiary, at Ludwig Maximilian University, Munich. She gained her Dr. Phil. in 1989. She has worked as in-house lawyer for Bertelsmann Buch AG and Amazon.com. In 1998 she became General Partner in Vivil GmbH und Co. KG, Offenburg. She is Founder and Chair of the Convoco Foundation. As Editor of Convoco! Editions she has published among others: *New Global Alliances: Institutions, Alignments and Legitimacy in the Contemporary World* (Convoco! Editions 2021), *The Standing of Europe* *in the New Imperial World Order* (Convoco! Editions, 2020), *The Multiple Futures of Capitalism* (Convoco! Editions, 2019), *The Common Good in the 21st Century* (Convoco! Editions, 2018), *Authority in Transformation* (Convoco! Editions, 2017), *Power and its Paradoxes* (Convoco! Editions, 2016), *To Do or Not To Do—Inaction as a Form of Action* (Convoco! Editions, 2015), *Dealing with Downturns: Strategies in Uncertain Times* (Convoco! Editions, 2014). In 2019 Corinne Flick became the Chair of the Board of Ambassadors at the ESMT Berlin.

Prof. Dr. Dr. h.c. Clemens Fuest (b. 1968) is President of the ifo Institute—Leibniz Institute for Economic Research at the University of Munich e.V., Executive Director of CESifo GmbH, Professor of Economics and Public Finance at Ludwig Maximilian University, Munich, and Director of the Center for Economic Studies (CES) at LMU.

He is among other posts a member of the Advisory Board to the German Federal Ministry of Finance and the Franco-German Board of Economic Experts, the European Academy of Sciences and Arts, as well as the Advisory Board of Ernst & Young GmbH. He is a member of the Scientific Advisory Board of the Market Economy Foundation (Kronberger Kreis) and the Foundation for Family Businesses in Germany and Europe. From August 2018 to August 2021 he was President of the IIPF (International Institute of Public Finance e.V.). In 2013 he received the Gustav Stolper Award of the Verein für Socialpolitik (Social Policies Society, VfS), and in 2019 he received the Hanns Martin Schleyer Award for 2018. In 2017 Clemens Fuest received an honorary doctorate from the Karlsruhe Institute of Technology (KIT). His research areas are economic and financial policy, international taxation, tax policy, and European integration. Before his appointment at Munich he was a professor at the Universities of Cologne (2001–08), Oxford (2008–13), and Mannheim (2013–16). He is the author of a number of books and has published many commentaries and byline articles on contemporary questions of economic policy in national and international journals. He also writes for newspapers such as *Handelsblatt, Frankfurter Allgemeine Zeitung, Die Zeit, Süddeutsche Zeitung, WirtschaftsWoche, Financial Times,* and *The Wall Street Journal.*

Prof. Dr. Birke Häcker holds the statutory Chair in Comparative Law at the University of Oxford. Since her appointment in 2016, she has been a Professorial Fellow at Brasenose College and in 2018 became the Director of Oxford's Institute of European and

Comparative Law. Prior to taking up her position, she was, *inter alia*, a Fellow of All Souls College, Oxford, and a Senior Research Fellow at the Max Planck Institute for Tax Law and Public Finance in Munich. As an undergraduate, she obtained a dual legal education, reading jurisprudence at Oxford as well as German law at the Universities of Tübingen and Bonn. Her Oxford D.Phil. was on comparative private law. She publishes on a broad range of topics in English and German private law, comparative law, and legal history.

Martha Jungwirth was born in 1940 in Vienna, where she continues to live and work. In 1961, while a student at the Academy of Applied Arts (1956–63), she was awarded the Msgr. Otto Mauer Prize, followed by the Theodor Körner Prize (1964) and the Joan Miró Prize (1966). Having studied under Professor Carl Unger, she later taught at the Academy of Applied Arts in Vienna 1967–77. She was a co-founder and the only female member of the Viennese collective- *Wirklichkeiten* (Realities), alongside Wolfgang Herzig, Kurt Kocherscheidt, Peter Pongratz, Franz Ringel, and Robert Zeppel-Sperl, whose work was shown in the exhibition at the Secession, Vienna, in 1968, curated by Otto Breicha. The group exhibited together from 1968 to 1972 and, in 1977, Jungwirth was included in documenta 6 in Kassel. In 2010, an entire room was dedicated to her work in the exhibition curated by Albert Oehlen for the Essl Museum, Klosterneuburg. A career retrospective spanning five decades was shown at the Kunsthalle Krems in 2014, followed by an exhibition focusing on her watercolors at the Kunstmuseum Ravensburg in 2018. That same year, she received the prestigious Oskar Kokoschka Prize awarded by the Austrian state, accompanied by an extensive solo exhibition at the Albertina in Vienna. A retrospective at the Museum Liaunig in Neuhaus marked the occasion of the artist's 80th birthday in 2020. In 2021 Martha Jungwirth was awarded the Grand Austrian State Prize, the Republic's highest commendation for an outstanding life's work in the field of art.

Dr. Bruno Kahl is President of the Bundesnachrichtendienst [German Federal Intelligence Service]. 1983: Law studies in Bonn, Germany, and in Lausanne, Switzerland. 1988: First state examination in law. 1991: Legal clerkships in Bonn and Speyer, Germany, and in Sydney, Australia. 1994: second state examination in law. 1995: Desk officer in the Federal Chancellery, and from 1996 Expert consultant in the CDU/CSU parliamentary group in the Bundestag. 2005: Head of the Minister's Office and spokesman for

Federal Minister Dr. Wolfgang Schäuble in the Federal Ministry of the Interior. 2006: Head of the Executive Group at the Federal Ministry of the Interior. 2010: Head of the Executive Group at the Federal Ministry of Finance. 2011: Head of Division VIII (in charge of privatizations, investments, and federal real estate) at the Federal Ministry of Finance until transfer to the Bundesnachrichtendienst in 2016.

Prof. Dr. Stefan Korioth gained his doctorate in law in 1990 and completed his postdoctoral qualification in public and constitutional law. From 1996 to 2000 he was Professor of Public Law, Constitutional History, and Theory of Government at the University of Greifswald. In 2000 he accepted the Chair of Public and Ecclesiastical Law at Ludwig Maximilian University, Munich. His publications include *Integration und Bundesstaat* (1990), *Der Finanzausgleich zwischen Bund und Ländern* (1997), *Grundzüge des Staatskirchenrechts* (with B. Jean d'Heur, 2000), *Das Bundesverfassungsgericht* (with Klaus Schlaich, 12th edition, 2021), and *Staatsrecht I* (5th edition, 2020).

Prof. Dr. Jörn Leonhard is Chair of Western European History at the Albert Ludwig University of Freiburg, and an author. Having studied history, political science, and German philology in Heidelberg and Oxford, he received his Ph.D. in 1998 and completed his postdoctoral qualification at Heidelberg University in 2004. From 1998 to 2003 he was a Fellow and Tutor at Oxford University; Visiting Research Fellow at the Alexander von Humboldt Foundation in the German–American Center for Visiting Scholars in Washington, D.C. in 2001; Fellow of the Royal Historical Society London since 2002; and Senior Fellow at the Institute for Contemporary History of the Historisches Kolleg in Munich from 2016 to 2017. From 2007 to 2012 he was Director of the School of History at the Freiburg Institute for Advanced Studies (FRIAS) and in 2012/13 Visiting Professor at Harvard University. His research and publications have received multiple awards. His most recent English publication is *Pandora's Box: A History of the First World War* (2018). Jörn Leonhard has been full member of the Heidelberg Academy of Sciences and Humanities since 2015 and Honorary Fellow of Wadham College, Oxford University, since 2019.

Prof. Dr. h.c. Rudolf Mellinghoff leads the Centre for the Digitalization of Tax Law (LMUDigiTax) at LMU Munich and is Scientific Director of the Institut Finanzen und Steuer e.V. (ifst). He studied at the

University of Münster and served his postgraduate legal internship in Baden-Württemberg. Between 1984 and 1987 he was a Research Assistant at the University of Heidelberg, becoming a Judge in the Finance Court of Düsseldorf in 1987. From 1987 to 1991 he was a Research Fellow at the Federal Constitutional Court. He was appointed Judge at the Finance Court of Düsseldorf in 1989. Rudolf Mellinghoff was Head of Department at the Ministry of Justice of Mecklenburg-Vorpommern between July 1991 and June 1992, and was appointed Presiding Judge of the Finance Court in 1996. In a second full-time position, he served as Judge of the Higher Administrative Court of Mecklenburg-Vorpommern between 1992 and 1996. From 1995 to 1996 he was also a member of the Constitutional Court of Mecklenburg-Vorpommern, and from 1997 to 2001 served as Judge at the German Federal Court of Auditors. From January 2001 to October 2011 Rudolf Mellinghoff served as Justice in the Second Senate of the Federal Constitutional Court. He then served as the President of the Federal Court of Auditors until July 2020. In 2006 Rudolf Mellinghoff was awarded an Honorary Doctorate from the University of Greifswald, and in 2007 from the Eberhard Karls University in Tübingen. In 2011 he was awarded the Grand Merit Cross with Star and Sash of the Order of Merit of the

Federal Republic of Germany. From 2009 to 2011 he was President of the German Section of the International Commission of Jurists, becoming Vice-President in 2012. He was Chair of the Deutsche Steuerjuristische Gesellschaft 2011 to 2017 and Vice Chair in 2018. Currently, Rudolf Mellinghoff is Chair of the Advisory Council of the Berliner Steuergespräche e.V., Chair of the Judicial Integrity Group, member of the Permanent Scientific Committee of the International Fiscal Association (FIA), and member of the European Academy of Sciences and Arts (Academia Scientiarum et Artium Europaea).

Prof. Dr. Timo Meynhardt holds the Dr. Arend Oetker Chair of Business Psychology and Leadership at the HHL Leipzig Graduate School of Management. He is Managing Director of the Center for Leadership and Values in Society at the University of St. Gallen, where he obtained his doctorate and postdoctoral qualification in business administration. For several years, he was Practice Expert at McKinsey & Company. Timo Meynhardt's work focuses on public value management and leadership, combining psychology and business management in his research and teaching. He is co-developer of the Leipzig leadership model and co-publisher of the *Public Value Atlas* for Switzerland

and Germany, which aims at making transparent the social benefits of companies and organizations (www.gemeinwohlatlas.de; www.gemeinwohl.ch). His Public Value Scorecard provides a management tool to measure and analyze the creation of public value. He is also Co-founder and Jury Member of the Public Value Awards for Startups.

Hans Ulrich Obrist (b. 1968, Zurich, Switzerland) is Artistic Director of the Serpentine Galleries in London, Senior Advisor at LUMA Arles, and Senior Artistic Advisor at The Shed in New York. Prior to this, he was the Curator of the Musée d'Art Moderne de la Ville de Paris. Since his first show "World Soup (The Kitchen Show)" in 1991, he has curated more than 350 exhibitions, his recent shows include "IT'S URGENT" at LUMA Arles (2019–21), and "Enzo Mari" at Triennale Milano (2020).

In 2011 Obrist received the CCS Bard Award for Curatorial Excellence, and in 2015 he was awarded the International Folkwang Prize, and most recently he was honored by the Appraisers Association of America with the 2018 Award for Excellence in the Arts.

Obrist's recent publications include *Ways of Curating* (2015), *The Age of Earthquakes* (2015), *Lives of the Artists, Lives of Architects* (2015), *Mondialité* (2017),

Somewhere Totally Else (2018), The *Athens Dialogues* (2018), *An Exhibition Always Hides Another Exhibition* (2019), *Maria Lassnig: Letters* (2020), *Entrevistas Brasileiras: Volume 2* (2020), *The Extreme Self: Age of You* (2021), and *Remember Nature* (2021).

Prof. Dr. Philipp Pattberg is Director of the Amsterdam Sustainability Institute (ASI), a platform for interdisciplinary research collaboration among all faculties at Vrije Universiteit Amsterdam. His current research analyzes options for institutional innovation to help accelerate the sustainability transition. Philipp Pattberg is author, co-author, or editor of eight books, 50 articles published in peer-reviewed journals, and 45 chapters in academic books, along with more than 80 papers, reports, and contributions to policy-oriented journals. His most recent book is *The Anthropocene Debate in Political Science* (co-edited with Thomas Hickmann, Sabine Weiland, and Lena Partzsch [Routledge 2018]). Since 2016, Philipp Pattberg has served as General Director of the Netherlands Research School for Socio-Economic and Natural Sciences of the Environment (SENSE). He is a senior research fellow of the international Earth System Governance Project. In the past, he has served as Chair of the Board of the Global Environmental Change Section of the German

Political Science Association between 2006 and 2010, as deputy-director of the Global Governance Project between 2006 and 2011, and as a member of the Management Committee member in the EU COST Action "Ocean Governance." Earlier professional or visiting affiliations included the American University (Washington D.C.), the Freie Universität Berlin, the London School of Economics and Political Science (LSE), Sciences Po Bordeaux, and TU Darmstadt. His work has been recognized with various scholarships, grants, and awards.

Prof. Dr. Herbert A. Reitsamer is a Professor of Neuro- and Sensory Physiology, and Professor of Ophthalmology and Optometry. He is Chairman of the University Eye Clinic Salzburg, Head of the Research Program in Experimental Ophthalmology and Vice-Rector for Innovation and Digitalization at Paracelsus Medical University. Prof. Reitsamer lectures in neurophysiology, the higher and integrative functions of the central nervous system, and ophthalmology. He is a member of Salzburg's Ethics Committee, Executive Board member of the Austrian Ophthalmological Society, and a member of the European Academy of Sciences. He is Chair of Ophthalmology at the Open Medical Institute and President of the Austrian

Chapter Affiliate of the American Association for Research in Vision and Ophthalmology. He is also a member of numerous advisory boards in universities, start-ups, and industrial enterprises; a member of editorial boards; and acts as referee for scientific journals and funding institutions.

Prof. Dr. Monika Schnitzer is Professor of Comparative Economics at the Ludwig Maximilian University, Munich (LMU). She has been a member of the German Council of Economic Experts since April 2020. Monika Schnitzer received her doctorate and postdoctoral qualification at the University of Bonn and was visiting researcher at Boston University, the MIT, Stanford University, Yale University, the University of California, Berkeley, and Harvard University. From 2006 to 2009, she was Dean of the Faculty of Economics at LMU. Her research focuses on innovation, competition, and multinational corporations. Her work has been published in the *American Economic Review*, in the *American Economic Journal: Economic Policy* and in the *Journal of the European Association*, among others.

Monika Schnitzer has been active in policy consulting for more than 20 years. Since 2001, she has been a member of the Board of Academic Advisors to the Federal Minister for Economic Affairs and Climate Action. From 2011 to 2019 she was Deputy Chair of the Expert Commission for Research and Innovation. She is currently a member of the Economic Advisory Group on Competition Policy of the General Directory "Competition" of the European Commission. Monika Schnitzer was elected a member of the Bavarian Academy of Science in 2008, and a member of the Academia Europaea in 2016. Since 2008 she has been a Fellow of the European Economic Association. From 2015 to 2016 she was Chairperson of the Verein für Socialpolitik, the German Economic Association. In 2005 she was awarded the Federal Order of Merit on Ribbon and, in 2012, the Bavarian Order of Merit.

Prof. Dr. Sven Simon is Chair of International Law, European Law, and Public Law at the Philipps University Marburg and since 2019 a Member of the European Parliament. Born in 1978, he studied law at the Justus Liebig University Gießen and at the University of Warwick, UK. He completed the first state legal examination in 2005 and received his doctorate in 2009. Following his practical legal training in Frankfurt, Berlin, Tel Aviv, and New York, he finished his second state legal examination in 2010. Sven Simon then returned to the Justus Liebig University Gießen to work as Academic Advisor for five years. In 2015 he was awarded his postdoctoral qualification for work on constitutional law analyzing the limits of the German Federal Court in the European integration process. After visiting professorships at the Free University Berlin and the University of Wisconsin, USA, he went on to an appointment at the Philipps University Marburg in 2016. Sven Simon is Deputy Chair of the United Nations Association of Germany.

Prof. Dr. Claudia Wiesner is Jean Monnet Chair and Professor for Political Science at Fulda University of Applied Sciences and Adjunct Professor in Political Science at Jyväskylä University. She leads several international research projects and networks and is Executive Director of the newly founded research institute Point Alpha e.V. In addition, she has been a Visiting Fellow at such institutions as the Center for European Studies at Harvard University, the Berlin Social Studies Centre, and the Robert Schumann Centre for Advanced Studies at the European University Institute (EUI). Her main research interests lie in the comparative study of democracy in the EU and its Member States, comparative research into policy innovations, and model projects and key concepts in political science. Recent publications include:

The European Central Bank between the Financial Crisis and Populisms (Palgrave Macmillan), with Corrado Macchiarelli, Mara Monti, and Sebastian Diessner, and *Rethinking Politicisation in Politics, Sociology and International Relations* (Palgrave Macmillan) edited by Claudia Wiesner.

Dr. Peter Wittig has been "Senior Advisor Global Affairs" for a global German industrial company since 2020. He is a Fellow of the Harvard Kennedy School and teaches as an Honorary Professor at Georgetown University in Washington, D.C. Previously, he was a member of the German Diplomatic Service for nearly four decades, holding a total of five ambassadorial posts. Most recently, he was German ambassador to London (2018–20), to Washington (2014–18), and to the United Nations in New York (2009–14). Ambassador Wittig studied history, political science, and law at the universities of Bonn, Freiburg, Canterbury, and Oxford. He then taught for three years at the University of Freiburg.

Hildegard Wortmann was born in Münster. After graduating as a state-certified foreign language correspondent and studying business administration at the University of Münster, Hildegard Wortmann started her career at Unilever in 1990. She held various positions there including Product and Brand Manager and was later Marketing Director for Calvin Klein. During her work with the company she gained international experience, including London and New York. Alongside her professional career she completed an MBA in London. In 1998 she moved to the BMW Group, where she led the relaunch of the MINI brand as Head of Brand Communication. Her other professional positions at BMW included marketing pre-development, innovation projects, product management, and after-sales. From 2010 to 2017 she was responsible for global product management for BMW. In addition, from 2016 she assumed overall brand responsibility for the BMW brand. With the development and launch of the electric brand BMW i, Hildegard Wortmann placed a decisive focus on e-mobility. In January 2018 she moved to Singapore, where she was responsible for the Asia-Pacific sales region. Hildegard Wortmann has been the Member of the Board of Management of AUDI AG for Sales and Marketing since July 1, 2019.

The CONVOCO! Forum 2021

The lectures and panel discussions of the CONVOCO! Forum "How much freedom must we forgo to be free?" on July 31, 2021, in Salzburg are available online.

Dr. Corinne Flick

Introduction

Prof. Dr. Andreas Reckwitz

Freedom and Coercion in the Late-Modern Culture of Self-Realization

Prof. Dr. Birke Häcker

Individual and Social Dimensions of Freedom and Liberty

Prof. Dr. Stefan Korioth, Prof. Dr. Jörn Leonhard, Prof. Dr. Timo Meynhardt, Prof. Dr. Philipp Pattberg, Prof. Dr. Claudia Wiesner

Panel I: Individual and Social Dimensions of Freedom and Liberty

Prof. Dr. Tim Crane

Freedom of Speech and Freedom of Thought

Prof. Dr. Monika Schnitzer

Competition as a Guarantor of Freedom

Prof. Dr. Dr. h.c. Clemens Fuest

Europe's Economy and the Conflict between the USA and China

Prof. Gabriel Felbermayr, Ph.D., Prof. Dr. Monika Schnitzer, Prof. Dr. Kai A. Konrad, Dr. Peter Wittig, Dr. Wolfgang Fink

Panel II: Europe's Economy and the Conflict between the USA and China

Prof. Dr. Sven Simon

Strains and Successes: The European Model of Freedom and the Conflict of Systems

Hans Ulrich Obrist & Martha Jungwirth

CONVOCO! Art Conversation

NEW GLOBAL ALLIANCES: INSTITUTIONS, ALIGNMENTS AND LEGITIMACY IN THE CONTEMPORARY WORLD *2021*

ISBN: 978-1-9163673-2-6

With contributions by: Maha Hosain Aziz, Bazon Brock, Garrett Wallace Brown, Udo Di Fabio, Clemens Fuest, Eugénia C. Heldt, Stefan Korioth, Jörn Leonhard, Rudolf Mellinghoff, Timo Meynhardt, Stefan Oschmann, Christoph G. Paulus, Gisbert Rühl, Wolfgang Schön, Sven Simon und Lothar H. Wieler

THE STANDING OF EUROPE IN THE NEW IMPERIAL WORLD ORDER *2020*

ISBN: 978-1-9163673-0-2

With contributions by: Fredrik Erixon, Gabriel Felbermayr, Birke Häcker, Matthias Karl, Parag Khanna, Kai A. Konrad, Stefan Korioth, Jörn Leonhard, Timo Meynhardt, Hans Ulrich Obrist with Edi Rama, Stefan Oschmann, Christoph G. Paulus, Rupprecht Podszun, Jörg Rocholl, Sven Simon, Yael Tamir, Roberto Viola, Claudia Wiesner

THE MULTIPLE FUTURES OF CAPITALISM *2019*

ISBN: 978-0-9931953-8-9

With contributions by: Lucio Baccaro, Jens Beckert, Bazon Brock, Corinne M. Flick, Sean Hagan, Kai A. Konrad, Stefan Korioth, Justin Yifu Lin, Rudolf Mellinghoff, Timo Meynhardt, Hans Ulrich Obrist with Adam Curtis, Stefan Oschmann, Christoph G. Paulus, Herbert A. Reitsamer, Albrecht Ritschl, Jörg Rocholl, Gisbert Rühl, Monika Schnitzer, Wolfgang Schön

THE COMMON GOOD IN THE 21st CENTURY *2018*

ISBN: 978-0-9931953-6-5

With contributions by: Roland Berger, Bazon Brock, Udo Di Fabio, Carl Benedikt Frey, Clemens Fuest, Kai A. Konrad, Stefan Korioth, Rudolf Mellinghoff, Timo Meynhardt, Hans Ulrich Obrist with Hito Steyerl and Matteo Pasquinelli, Stefan Oschmann, Christoph G. Paulus, Jörg Rocholl, Wolfgang Schön, Jens Spahn

AUTHORITY IN TRANSFORMATION *2017*

ISBN: 978-0-9931953-4-1

POWER AND ITS PARADOXES *2016*

ISBN: 978-0-9931953-2-7

TO DO OR NOT TO DO—INACTION AS A FORM OF ACTION *2015*

ISBN: 978-0-9931953-0-3

DEALING WITH DOWNTURNS: STRATEGIES IN UNCERTAIN TIMES *2014*

ISBN: 978-0-9572958-8-9

COLLECTIVE LAW-BREAKING—A THREAT TO LIBERTY *2013*

ISBN: 978-0-9572958-5-8

WHO OWNS THE WORLD'S KNOWLEDGE? *2012*

ISBN: 978-0-9572958-0-3

CAN'T PAY, WON'T PAY? SOVEREIGN DEBT AND THE CHALLENGE OF GROWTH IN EUROPE *2011*

ISBN: 978-0-9572958-3-4

www.ingramcontent.com/pod-product-compliance
Lightning Source LLC
Chambersburg PA
CBHW020243030426
42336CB00010B/591